Dr. Sheila Graham Smith is a retired executive faculty member of Baylor University. Her professional work encompassed advocacy for students with special needs. Her Master's degree is in Educational Psychology and her Doctorate is in Curriculum and Instruction. She was the Director of the Disability Support Office at Baylor University. Dr. Smith was also instrumental in founding the disability support program in Beirut, Lebanon called SKILD (Special Kids with Individual Learning Differences), a beacon educational program in the Middle East. She was born and raised in Beirut and considers herself bilingual and bicultural, arriving in the United States in the early 1970s. A mother of two and a grandmother of five, she lives in Waco, Texas. In addition to being an author, she is an avid organic gardener, blogger, and cook.

Best wishes on your journey,

D. Sheila G. Smith

This book is dedicated to my grandchildren, Kate, Natalie, Jack, Luke, and Kendall, who daily inspire me to be my best self.

Dr. Sheila Graham Smith

TELL THE TRUTH ABOUT ADULTERY

A Story of Love, Betrayal, and Hope

AUSTIN MACAULEY PUBLISHERS™

LONDON • CAMBRIDGE • NEW YORK • SHARJAH

Ordering Information:
Quantity sales: special discounts are available on quantity purchases by corporations, associations, and others. For details, contact the publisher at the address below.

Publisher's Cataloging-in-Publication data
Smith, Dr. Sheila Graham
Tell the Truth About Adultery: A Story of Love, Betrayal, and Hope

ISBN 9781643782423 (Paperback)
ISBN 9781643782430 (Hardback)
ISBN 9781643782447 (Kindle e-book)
ISBN 9781645367277 (ePub e-book)

Library of Congress Control Number: 2019937778

The main category of the book — Family & relationships / Divorce & Separation

www.austinmacauley.com/us

First Published (2019)
Austin Macauley Publishers LLC
40 Wall Street, 28th Floor
New York, NY 10005
USA

mail-usa@austinmacauley.com
+1 (646) 5125767

Thank you to the army of women who've marched alongside me:

Elaine White, who helped me hone my words for this book.

Linda Dulin whose own story gave me courage to find my voice.

Leslie Smith, a stalwart friend from college years till today who was always on call for whatever emergency through this process of healing.

Barbara Hamlin, my creative 'bestie' whose photographs inspired the cover of this book.

Ibtissam Constantine, my childhood friend who completely gets me!

My three sisters, Catherine, Rose Mary, and Christine, the glue that bonds this crazy family together, on whose honest support and unconditional love I depend.

And most importantly, my graciously generous, elegantly formidable mother who pulled out the best in her children.

Introduction Letter from My Sixty-Plus Self

It has been twenty years since I wrote my divorce story! Back then, I had sent it to a publishing company, and they were initially interested. However, the editorial board rescinded their interest and responded to me with an unusually worded sentence,

"We think the raw emotions you express would be too difficult to read. No, we are not interested in publishing your story at this time." So, I put it away till now.

A new friend in my life, a fellow writer, was asking me about my past and in getting to know each other, I mentioned that I had written this mini saga down. She was anxious to read it. Her response after reading *Tell the Truth About Adultery* was the antithesis of the editorial board's opinion.

She said, "This is authentic and poignant. Other women who have experienced what you have need to read it."

Yes, twenty years ago, I wrote this for me, for my healing, but I also had others in mind who might have walked in my shoes and needed validation, to be seen and feel safe in their vulnerability, to know that their feelings and experiences were authentic and not 'too' anything!

Considering the '#metoo' movement in our world today, I want women, especially minister's wives who find themselves in similar situations, to be brave about their stories. Men in positions of power in the entertainment and political spheres are being exposed. My prediction that the spiritual arena is next is coming to fruition. I urge victimized women to no longer believe the lies by which they've been manipulated in the past when their thoughts were held captive by their abuser. Tell your story and begin the process of healing. Be challenged. As your sisters hear your story, they will be encouraged and strengthened.

I'm now in my sixties and have remained silent, except for in private conversations. Recently, I've experienced a reawakening that's been in part a settling for the status-quo and another part reinvention. For you see, in the last twenty years, I have gone through major life upheavals as we all do. Right after my divorce, my father and brother died within five years of each other, I remarried the loveliest man (a childhood friend), fought illnesses (hepatitis C, lupus, and breast cancer), became a grandmother (five exuberant times), had to take early medical retirement from a hard, sought-for career and claim disability, and mourned my mother's recent passing. Whew! It's been quite a ride! On the bright side, marrying my best friend during tumult has been a startling and precious gift. He has been a true partner, only wishing what is best for me.

A variable in this roller coaster litany of upheavals is the autoimmune disorder, lupus. I've experienced numerous hospital stays and procedures, convalesced and recuperated. And I can say truthfully that I've now settled into a place of peace, working each day within the job description of being healthy. Practically, I've learned that my responsibility is to do whatever is in my power to be as healthy as possible. Spiritually, I'm learning to live one day at a time with a recurrent request of God, "Put in my path, show me today, what you want of me."

What does this repeating request look like? It's living in the mindset of recognition, recognizing God's voice, acknowledging his direction, and following through. These daily implementations are not extraordinary! Sometimes it's as simple as turning the compost pile and collecting eggs from our hens. Other days it's saying 'yes' to a tutoring request from students who've been referred to me. It's always about sharing meals with friends and family. It's about holding babies in the church nursery so that young parents are free to soak up much-needed spiritual nourishment.

It's about spending endless hours in my garden and opening the garden gate to friends and neighbors. It's about writing devotionals as part of our church's ministry. It's writing bi-weekly blog posts. I've learned to be grateful for forced medical retirement because how else would I have had time to pick up grandchildren from school and offer uninterrupted hours of grandma presence? Chronic illness sifts away the debris of life's distractions. What's left are the essentials: relationships and the love needed to grow these relationships.

In reading back on my story from twenty years ago and being my sixty-plus self today, I feel like the gnarly old olive tree referred to in Psalms 52:8.

"For I'm like a spreading olive tree in God's house; for I trust in God's true love forever and ever."

I remember as a little girl the sprawling silver leafed olive trees surrounding our home on a terraced hillside in Lebanon. What does an olive tree look like? Some are hundreds of years old and so large that a child like me could climb their knobby protrusions like a ladder and nestle into welcoming branches with a good book to read or just for imaginary play.

From the viewpoint of a child, twenty years seemed like an eternity back then. Yet, I didn't even wait twenty years to get married! As an extremely young adult, nineteen, I idealistically assessed myself as mature and ready for marriage. I married between my sophomore and junior years in college and had children at twenty-three and twenty-four. Yes, my boys were twelve months apart! Back then in the seventies, getting married and having a family young was the norm.

As girls in the Church, we were raised under the tutelage of outspoken Christian leaders who espoused the mandate that a man, a male, was the head of a household. The Christian conference and revival speakers taught a hierarchal system of marriage in which the female was under the auspices of the male husband. And heaven forbid if you were single, because then you were still under the authority of your father or considered a freakish independent female. We were the generation that had the audacity to demand a place in the workforce, never dreaming of the day of receiving equal pay to our male peers!

A good Christian wife was to sublimate her intellect, her emotions, her desires, and her gifts, to never out-shine her husband. If she had the temerity to do so, she was negatively considered as being pushy, aggressive, and conceited. The same attributes in a male were viewed as desirable and tangible proof of admirable leadership qualities. This pattern was not only acted out in church circles, but in society at large. It was an atmosphere ripe for spousal abuse. Remnants of this teaching still permeate Christian circles today. That is another reason why I am now convinced that resuscitating this twenty-year-old story is appropriately timely. I want my granddaughters to grow into their full potential and not be repressed by a story that was not told, my adultery and divorce story, my younger-self story.

The familiar old chorus that we, women of the mid-twentieth century, sang in our church congregations needs to remain an old song. Let's not repeat that old familiar chorus where we remain silent and, in our silence, perpetuate the tune that abuse is OK. By telling our stories, we uncover the secrets, expose the crippling pretentious religious constructs, and free our grandchildren to thrive in their marriages. I want my granddaughters to glory in transparent and honest marriages where they can pursue their passions and dreams without the fearful shackles of outshining their spouses. I want my grandsons to love their wives in such a way as to inspire growth in mutual celebration of gifts, to flourish in vulnerable love. Maybe by telling my old but familiar story, other women will be validated and embrace the courage to tell their own truth.

Prologue

Be gracious to me,
Oh God,
be gracious;
for I have made thee my refuge.
I will take refuge in the shadow of thy wings
until the storms are past.
I will call upon God Most High,
on God who fulfills his purpose for me.
He will send his truth and his love that never fails.
Psalms 57:1–3

I have read every book out there on divorce. There are at least fifteen sitting on my shelf in the den. I'm trying to understand this crazy wind tunnel through which I have been forced to tumble. Some days, my spiritual bearings serve me well. And when thrown against the walls of anger, grief, and disappointment, somehow the impact doesn't knock me completely off balance, just a tumble in an intermittent dizzy spell. Those are the good days. Other days find me sucked along in a tornado of emotions where everything is out of kilter, where mentally I know God is in control, but I'm certainly not feeling it.

I could relate smidgens of wisdom given to me by divorce authors writing out of their pain of divorce, or counselors and other professionals sharing experiences as healers, yet a major element was missing. What does a Christian woman, who has been dumped, do?

Yes, our circumstances are unique. We, like our other sisters, idealistically strode through our first marriages, confident in God's chosen man for us, never doubting that our husbands meant every word of their noble hopes and promises carried in our ceremonial vows. We held our heads high because nothing could be purer, and more honor-bound than being a Christian man's wife. I walked confidently down that aisle anticipating a full life of being cherished because I knew how to be the wife of a servant of God. (Oh, the idealism of youth!)

I mean, who better to serve in that role? Like the apostle Paul who boasted of his credentials, I too did likewise. Born of missionary parents, with grandparents as stalwarts in the faith, the youngest of five children, all eagerly and unflinchingly living the Godly life, having committed my life to serve the Lord at an early age, eagerly volunteering to teach Sunday School, Vacation Bible School, and Training Union, opting to attend services at a local orphanage during college years instead of attending a glitzy church...and the list goes on and on. What a vain list! What an inconsequential list!

Hadn't I always done everything a good Christian girl should at each turn? And now, the crowning glory—I was to be a pastor's wife! Life couldn't be better! And it was glorious, I thought. There wasn't a church, assignment, or mission field in which I didn't bask. The kicker was that I thought my husband, I'll call him Sam, and I were of like mind, soul, and heart. We went to the mission field together with our young boys, living out our heart's desire, standing on the Psalmist's promise that if we acknowledged our heavenly father in all things, He would grant us our heart's desire. Speaking of the condition of the heart, I remember as an engaged couple sitting on Sam's grandmother's couch where we did most of our courting, reading Psalm 139, promising to memorize it, and claiming it as our Psalm, our motto, our creed for life. Where did that standard go? How can sleeping with another woman and "not being able to help falling in love with another," jive with the plea of "Search me O' God and know my heart. Test me and know my anxious thoughts. See if there is any offensive way in me and lead me in the way everlasting?"

What happened? I guess I will always ask that question, and I don't have any answers.

This book is not about answers to questions of "What did I do wrong?" But, this book is an honest and raw attempt at saying, "You are not alone." I look at it as laying my deepest insecurities, dashed hopes, and ugliest fears out on the finger painting table of nursery school and letting all of my Christian sisters smear the concoction around, spreading our fingers in each other's divorce and betrayal times, touching elbows, crossing over boundaries, getting paint on each other, and maybe coming up with a new and conjoint piece of art—a fresh vignette composed of all our lost love experiences.

I just want to share with other wives who have found themselves in my shoes of pain, anger, and hope. Maybe in sharing with each other, we can somehow survive our journeys and hold our heads up high again, confident in God's love, knowing we are worth not throwing away after all.

Silence

Chapter 1

Who can find a capable wife?
Her sons with one accord call her happy,
her husband too, and he sings her praises
Many a woman shows how capable she is,
but you excel them all.
Charm is delusion and beauty fleeting;
it is the God-fearing woman who is honored.
Extol her for the fruit of all her toil,
and let her labors bring her honor in the city gate.
Proverbs 31: 10, 28–31

I had lost all honor, respect, and confidence in myself. Divorce has a way of doing that to you. And betrayal strips off that coat of respect almost beyond mending. I had seemingly failed as a wife. And I had certainly failed in the eyes of my church and family. For as my ex-mother-in-law put it, "A husband doesn't go looking outside of the home unless he isn't getting his needs met at home. Don't say anything to anybody, Sheila. Just keep quiet and eventually he will come back." That was the sage advice of my parents-in-law when I sought them out for counsel. The time of silence began.

Can you remember back when you were a little girl? What did you get in trouble for the most? I mean, what did your parents emphasize as being the worst thing you could possibly do? With me, it was lying. Telling the truth was expected and punishment always came easier if we confessed first. I remember distinctly chaffing through lectures on telling the truth, dreading the inevitable outcome of my lying about something or other. In other words, telling the truth was drilled into me from way back when. Therefore, being honest about telling my truth about this pain of divorce was something that I was compelled to do, no matter what the consequences.

In *Ephesians*, the author tells us to: "Throw off falsehood; speak the truth to each other, for all of us are the parts of one body." (How much more so within the bounds of marriage) "If you are angry," he continues, "do not let anger lead you into sin; do not let sunset find you still nursing it; leave no loop-hole for the devil." My sunset time of silence had begun and to come out at dawn a whole and halfway sane person, I had to tell the truth about my divorce. Bear with me, fellow sister in Christ, and see if my pain can go beyond condolences for you.

In being honest about pain, I must state a terrifying truth for me; this world of divorce is not a safe and secure place. Betrayal really does happen, and it can happen to anybody.

In the initial throes of being rejected, I was in desperate shock. I felt as though I had been touched by and smeared with something inexpressibly filthy—the insides of another woman had been physically, intricately, and intimately placed within me. It was no longer an intuition that was telling me something and that I must run. It was now a fact, but oh, how I wanted to run and run and never stop.

Let me tell you of the first chapter of confession on Sam's part. We came home from that ill-fated date. I alternated in my hysteria from beating my fists on his chest and cursing him and his new lover, to groveling, begging, and pleading for another chance.

Funny thing is, as a couple, as a pastor and wife, we used to lead marriage enrichment seminars, and one of our nuggets of advice was to have a scheduled regular date night each week! We had been on one of those dates, but this one was different. This one indelibly marked the time and place forever as the place where Sam confessed his current affair. He subsequently had the confidence and temerity to present me with a pros and cons list, a sheet of paper divided down the middle itemizing her, Terry's, attributes and my corresponding faults! I pathetically accepted this list as a valid assessment and promised to work hard at changing. I would become whatever he wanted. She was athletic, I would work out more aggressively. She was quiet, yet strong, I would tone down my exuberance. She was younger, I would…do nothing. She was outdoorsy, I would learn to hunt and shoot.

"Just tell me," I begged. "I will do anything. Just don't leave us."

Later, after coming home from the restaurant, Sam was sitting on our living room couch and I was crouched at his knees, hanging on and sobbing, desperately seeking a retraction of his words. "I can't help it if I love her," his responding words summed up the atrocious date night.

There began my gruesome quest for answers that plagued the next three months of survival. I wanted to know every detail of their relationship and the weird thing is that I got what I asked for. He told me the story: past, present, and his hopes for the future with her. I can remember telling him that I understood how she fell for him. Wasn't he kind, generous, and sympathetic? Didn't he know just the right thing to say to a broken heart and sad spirit? You see, Terry had recently been divorced from an abusive husband and was alone trying to raise precious twin daughters. I say precious because I recall how cute they looked Easter morning, dressed alike, mother and twin daughters, when I visited their church where Sam was interim pastor. I even told them so, obviously totally unaware as to whom I was speaking. She had moved back home with her parents, and my husband would visit her and her girls there. He said that he asked the mother's permission to continue seeing her daughter since she had recognized the growing attraction between them each Sunday.

Terry's mother facilitated their time alone. When he first began this interim pastorate, he never spent the night there, insisting he wanted to be home with us. Slowly, that began to change as he started leaving on Saturday afternoon and then eventually staying Sunday night as well. The church would put him up in the local motel. He told me that he was meeting with the deacons each Sunday night as they began earnestly seeking a full-time pastor. I never doubted a word. Why should I? He was my devoted husband of twenty-three years, so I thought.

As Sam recounted to me their story of courtship, he said that the first time they were together as lovers was a Sunday night after church. She had asked him that afternoon if he wanted her to come to his motel room in that small town that night. He affirmatively responded and so that the townspeople would not see her car parked at the motel, her mother dropped her off and picked her up at a prearranged time. The ensuing rendezvous times increased rapidly.

Sam's job during the week entailed a lot of traveling and he began using rent cars instead of claiming mileage on our vehicle. Again, Terry's mother was involved. She would drop her daughter off at prearranged locations across the state. They (Terry and my husband) would travel together and stay in motels and hotels easily without recognition in strange towns. Their lodgings and meals were already paid for with his travel expenses, so all the circumstances, including the fact that as a school teacher, Terry had the summer months off, served to cushion their affair well. Even childcare was of no consequence since grandma was helping. This type of enabling by Terry's mother even extended to one of our denomination's conventions. Terry was dropped off by her mom at the convention hotel where Sam audaciously kept her in his room. They apparently enjoyed a mini vacation at the expense of the seminary for which he worked.

How do I know all this? I know because he told me. Remember, I harassed him and harangued him with questions and was rewarded with answers! We had been each other's best friends so long that telling each other everything was a habit that was hard to break. During those three months of their active courtship, it might sound like I

19

rolled over and died, but I didn't. Yes, we did go to counseling and I acted on the counselor's advice. The counselor said, "Sheila, do you want him back out of a guilty conscience or do you want him back because he realizes how much he really does love you after all?" Of course, I wanted him back because he ultimately chose me. That question just spurred me on to work harder. I tried to lose weight and I wasn't even over weight! Isn't that what we women always resort to first? I bought sexy lingerie. I fixed tantalizing meals. I did know how to cook well!!! I remember asking him to go through my closet and weed out the clothes that he didn't like, as if clothes make a difference! That very week, the discarded clothes were packed up and taken to Salvation Army. How pathetic is that?

One weekend, in conjunction with our university's faculty conference, I planned a romantic get-away with candles, soft music, even a new nightgown that my sister, who as yet knew nothing about the affair, had helped me shop for and buy. I was convinced that if I worked at it hard enough, I could win him back. How did it go? Is wax melting all over my new gown and ruining it indicative of the state of affairs? Sam sexually responded to me during those attempts. And each time, I thought that I had won. But no, Terry was the winner. For he would say, "Yeah, that was good, but I wasn't thinking of you during all that."

I didn't give up. I had to try harder. I finally told my siblings and mother after this three-month time of silence, but no one else. The silence intensified. I know. When all else fails, try prayer. Maybe God's word, and not my sexual prowess, could be the weapon of battle. Sermons on Sunday morning became rewritten lessons for Sam. I would listen intently, take notes diligently, and re-tell the sermons to him when he returned from his trips. The response was predictable: "Quit preaching at me!"

As I continued the deteriorating downhill realization that my sweetheart, the love of my youth, the father of my boys, really didn't want me anymore, my body responded aggressively. I couldn't eat. Now that was a new phenomenon! I couldn't sleep. I would collapse from exhaustion a couple of hours a night. Each night, if I slept, my vivid dreams of the two of them making love together would jar me awake. By then, we were in separate bedrooms, his choice, not mine. I couldn't stand the thought of him sleeping in another room and in another bed, so I would sneak into his bed and slide up to his body warmth, shivering and shaking. I would beg him to hold me so that I could calm down and sleep again. He would oblige me.

When did I finally give up this foolish battle? One Friday, I had an appointment with a doctor to try and get to the bottom of my increasing body ailments. Sam had a weekend trip planned with Terry and her girls to Six Flags. He was so confident in his deception that he disguised the weekend as a student recruiting assignment and so was financed by the seminary, his employer. Again, Terry's mother facilitated the whole affair by dropping her daughter and granddaughters off to spend the weekend with their interim pastor, my husband, Terry's lover. I asked him if there was any way to cancel his trip and stay with me because I didn't want to go to the doctor alone. I feared the prognosis. He apologized and said, "Sheila, you know I can't do that. I've promised Terry and the girls this weekend and I can't disappoint her." My answer was silence again.

That very week, while we were driving to town, I told him that I finally realized what my worth was in his eyes. I had reached a tragic conclusion. Therefore, I was planning to see a lawyer. I was filing for divorce. I could not give him any more time to decide between his two women. Yes, I took that decision out of his hands and off his shoulders. He affirmed my decision when he said, "Remember, you're the one filing for divorce, not me. I'm willing to work on this. You're not."

Sam's idea of working on it was to stay married to me, keep his high-profile job, but continue to see Terry as a friend. He was so selfish that he couldn't fathom why such an arrangement wouldn't be acceptable to me! I finally spoke up and said, "You do what you need to do, and I'll do what I need to do."

Maybe that wasn't the right way to have handled things, but I couldn't take it anymore. The energy to fight had run out. I did see a lawyer that week and in that very same week, I found out that I had chronic hepatitis C. I had apparently contracted hepatitis C through a tainted blood transfusion after a previous hysterectomy. You see, I'm a genetic carrier for a blood clotting disorder, which dictates me having blood infusions before and after any surgical procedures. The diagnosis of hepatitis C was the answer to my broken body, but my broken heart had no answers. I wanted to scream at Sam. "Look what you have done to me, to us. You had so much and could have kept it, but you have thrown it all away."

Many times, as I felt the walls of my home caving in on me, I escaped into long walks. One poignant night, I walked and talked, stomped and screamed, cursed God and cursed that 'whore' who had stolen my husband. I begged and pleaded with the Lord to make things right again, but all I got back was silent clouds scurrying across a star-studded warm night. I wandered for hours apparently, for on my return, Sam was on the phone with Terry. "She's back. Don't worry, she's all right." I must have been gone for hours unaware. I stared at him with the phone gripped to his ear, walked into my room, and closed the door.

The suffocating silence and isolation increased. I used to wonder what thoughts possessed people who wished for death. For me, it wasn't being possessed by thoughts, but an overwhelming desire to sink into nothingness. I didn't want to think anymore. I just wanted to go to sleep and not wake up. Even just breathing proved to be too taxing. Yes, I did plan out several suicidal scenarios. One such disaster included me grabbing one of Sam's hunting rifles. But I'm so anti-gun that I had no clue how to operate it and just ended up throwing it down with defeated frustration.

Do you sometimes read the Psalms repeatedly just to hear your emotions echoed in the words of David? Now here was a man who totally messed up his life, yet still had a profound relationship with God. That is what I found out. No matter how depressed, I knew that my relationship with my heavenly father was still intact, maybe a bit skewed, but still secure. David, like me, had been raised right with good supportive parents teaching him that if you follow God's rules, all should go well. Where do we get this unattainable theology of righteousness always winning out?

Did you approach your early adult years in this cloud of euphoric idealism? I did, and I can definitely hear myself in the Psalmist's words, "Carefree as I was, I said, I can never be shaken. But, Lord, it was thy will to shake my mountain refuge; thou didst hide thy face, and I was struck with dismay. I called unto thee, O Lord, and I pleaded with thee, Lord, for mercy; what profit is in my death if I go down into the pit? Can the dust confess thee or proclaim thy truth? Hear, O Lord, and be gracious to me; Lord, be my helper. Thou hast turned my laments into dancing; thou hast stripped off my sackcloth and clothed me with joy, that my spirit may sing psalms to thee and never cease, I will confess thee forever, O Lord my God."

After Sam's continued confession of love for another, I felt like I was buried in a tomb of shock with the dirt and rubble of years of love smothering me. I thought I had the answers and now all I had was silence and shame. Wasn't I the pastor's wife, the missionary, the minister? Didn't I have a special dose of intuition and wisdom? Weren't scripture verses always pushing themselves forward in my psyche to render healing and aid to others?

Yet God seemed silent. I was silent. My scriptures were even hushed. The silence echoed in my mind, constricted my throat, and burned my eyes. If it wasn't for family and friends during the aftershock months, I really don't think I would have physically made it. And it was dear, sweet girlfriends and siblings that finally succeeded in jarring me into anger.

I aimed, like poison darts, all that I was towards God. At that point, it had become anger. I yelled at Him the truth of this reality of divorce in which I was floundering. I refused to abandon my passion and I held on to God with aggressive tears and doubts. You would think that one body would have had enough of tears! Those tears were my most plentiful and generous gifts to the Lord these days. They were my form of worship and prayer. At first, I could barely go an hour without crying.

Now, almost two years have passed, and I can go several days and sometimes even a week without letting go some grieving tears. And they flow when you least expect it, like in the grocery store watching a sweet old couple helping each other out as they maneuver around impatient young folks or try to decipher a label. I realize afresh while looking at them that I won't grow old with the husband of my youth.

Also, in the grocery store, I stand motionless watching a young couple giggle, touch, and share wanton looks as they pick out groceries for a special meal. That too brings a lump to my throat and tears puddle in my eyes. I remember that Sam and I used to enjoy grocery shopping together and planning neat meals for ourselves and friends. We used to love to entertain together. Then I wander off in my thoughts and wonder if they cook together, if Sam and Terry enjoy browsing through cookbooks, and having friends over. Do they have friends?

Tears came and come at different times and in weird places. Will the grieving never end? During the latter days of the silence span, when sleep escaped me incessantly, I would be on my knees crouching on the floor by the couch, holding on to the cushions like a life preserver as sobs racked my body. Those animal groans would be wrenched from my insides as I agonizingly hurled my grief and anger at God.

Now I know experientially what the author of *Hebrews* talked about when he described how far-reaching is the power of the word of God. I physically have felt that depth. "For the word of God is alive and active. It cuts more keenly than any two-edged sword, piercing as far as the place where life and spirit, joints and marrow, divide. It sifts the purposes and thoughts of the heart. There is nothing in creation that can hide from him; everything lies naked and exposed to the eyes of the One with whom we have to reckon." This kind of vulnerability, this kind of honesty is true worship. My visceral anger was worship, because I was communicating it to God!

Words didn't form my pleas and questions, just moans, cries, tears, and more tears. Sometimes, I would wake up still on my collapsed knees realizing that I had fallen asleep after all with my face flat against the damp cushion. It was during one of these uncontrollable crying spells that I heard the voice of the Lord. My name was spoken so clearly, "Sheila," that I was silenced, knowing immediately who called me by name. Though desperately lonely, I wasn't alone. I heard my master's voice, and it was enough to calm my fears for the present. That storm, that night, had passed.

Surely, I could go on for at least another day. I crawled up on the couch, pulled the afghan over me, and slept dreamlessly for several hours. Blessed dreamless sleep!

The next morning, while reading that day's devotional from *'My Utmost for His Highest,'* by Oswald Chambers, I read how Jesus' voice, when calling Mary's name in the Garden, calmed her fears and gave her direction for what to do that day. I claimed that personal miracle for myself!

Eventually, my husband left me and was trying out his new life with a new and improved model and new children. When his adultery and deception became public knowledge among his academic peers, he was terminated from his job at the university. My sons and I were left at home. I had to get up off my grieving bed and start being a mom again.

My children were attending the same university where Sam and I worked. My boys were good students and socially active as well. Because of the sudden loss of another income to facilitate their college years, I asked my sons to move back home. I lived right off campus, closer than their own boarding accommodations. I promised them total ease to come and go, to carry on their lives with as much freedom as they needed. In fact, our home became a favorite destination for their friends. They had late night study groups, impromptu suppers, pre-fraternity party 'get ready' happenings, and many just relaxed times in our large sprawling living room. I fondly remember one time on a rare school snow day when my boys and their friends collected large trash bags and spent a raucous day sledding around campus on any incline they could find.

Their makeshift sledding day culminated in a game night of charades at our home where I filled their bellies with massive quantities of homemade soup and biscuits. I remember also the time when I woke up in the wee hours of the morning to find a bleary-eyed gathering of students around the dining room table pulling an all-nighter exam study marathon. I cooked for them a breakfast of fortifying biscuits and gravy with a mountain of scrambled eggs. To this day, when I run across my sons' friends, they fondly reminisce and remind me of those now famous biscuits! With opportunities like these right in front of me, I took care of the business at hand, my boys. I tried to redirect my broken heart and instead expended energy on daily, immediate, and practical responsibilities.

Remember that passage of scripture telling us who are weary and worn to come to Him? Matthew 11:28 says, "Come to me, all whose work is hard, whose load is heavy, and I will give you relief. Bend your necks to my yoke and learn from me, for I am gentle and humble hearted; and your souls will find relief. For my yoke is good to bear, my load is light."

This does not mean that He will put you to bed and sing you a lullaby to sleep and keep a cool rag on your fevered brow. The opposite is valid. He will get you out of bed, put your feet on the floor, and put life back into your listless arms. This business of being half dead while you are still alive will eventually dissipate with God's infusion of purposefulness and fulfillment in the return of vital activity. Throw off the heavy blankets of pitiful righteous sanctimonious victimization. Bask instead in the invigorating shower of God's royal vitality.

Listen, my dear girlfriends, to what Isaiah experienced. "Do you not know, have you not heard? The Lord, the everlasting God, creator of the wide world, grows neither weary nor faint; no man can fathom his understanding. He gives vigor to the weary, new strength to the exhausted. Young men may grow weary and faint. Even in their prime, they may stumble and fall, but those who look to the Lord will win new strength, they will grow wings like eagles; they will run and not be weary, they will march on and never grow faint." (Isaiah 40: 28–31)

I felt like a failure at being a wife, but no one was going to take away me being a mom. At one point, I had asked my husband how he could leave his boys. I could understand dissatisfaction with me and rejecting me, but his boys? How can you turn your back on two fine men like that? His answer was, "I've done my job of raising them. They're grown up now. They might not understand, but eventually, they'll come around."

That statement totally blew me away! I might no longer be a wife, but I would always be a mother, for better or for worse. Again and again, this conviction has stretched its kind fingers out to me, firmly grasped my hands, and placed them on my children to reconnect us once more. It is not that I had abdicated all responsibility in parenting, it's just that my diligence had stymied with lack of direction from the dank seemingly impenetrable fog of depression. I had been temporarily lost and confused, not able to see through self-pity and self-absorption.

For me, unknown tomorrows would continue to unfold with their own harrowing secrets and surprises. But I could be assured of God's instruction at each step, no matter how painful. You can do the same and allow others in similar circumstances, or those who have been through divorce, to buttress your steps in rebuilding a life as a single parent.

Pain

Chapter 2

After this, Job broke silence and cursed the day of his birth.
Why should the sufferer be born to see the light? Why is life
given to men who find it so bitter?
They wait for death, but it does not come,
they seek it more eagerly than hidden treasure.
They are glad when they reach the tomb,
and when they come to the grave, they exult.
Why should a man be born to wander blindly,
hedged in by God on every side?
My sighing is all my food,
and groans pour from me in a torrent.
Every terror that haunted me has caught up with me, and
all that I feared has come upon me. There is no peace of
mind nor quiet for me;
I chafe in torment and have no rest.
Job 3:1, 20–26

I can almost ask myself these questions objectively after two
Christmases alone—that is without my husband. What hurts
the most? Being replaced by a younger model, watching my
boys re-figure what love and family mean, or having my ex-
in-laws enfold the new wife with open arms? Who is this
new wife anyway? I can't help from thinking a caddy
vicious description of Terry. She is the one who went after
her preacher, the one who snuck all over the state with my
husband to sleep with him, and the one whose mother
connived and facilitated those rendezvous.

People say that it takes at least five years to get over the pain. It scabs over and turns into just another scar. After twenty-three years of marriage, five years seems a miserly pittance. It's obvious that I'm still angry and hurt even though I try to hide it from my family and friends who so desperately want me to be well. I vacillate between sincerely wishing Sam well and praying that he is finally content to conjuring up scenarios where the two of them are miserable and he ultimately confesses to what a horrible mistake he made. I need to set free all the resentment that is imploding inside of my caged up, brittle heart.

I can stay in that state of victimization or I can choose to work my way out of this tangle of emotions. Do you ever feel so tied up with pain that you want to call your ex up and make sure he understands exactly how much you hate him? Even that pain all wrapped up in barbed wire hate is a form of a comfort zone. It is an easy pattern to follow

...get up...face another day alone...wonder if he's miserable...hope he is miserable...feel justified by hatred ...go to bed hurting... pray for sleep...see another dawn of resentment. Are you trapped in that same cycle as well?

Do you find yourself bouncing between aggressively seeking out relationships and retreating furtively back to safety like a scared rabbit? My emotions want to protect my broken heart and simultaneously dart out, seeking new love. Yet, Christ continually calls us to attempt something beyond the comprehension of our emotions. We want to remain within our comfort zones of justifiable existence, whether we are justifying being victimized and act out of martyrdom or are justifying being righteous and act out of sanctimony. Christ asks us to dare to venture past the obvious living within our box of talent and dare to do the impossible (living alone) with Christ. We become the Holy Order of the Inadequate, totally relying on God's provision within each of our endeavors.

I had read in Romans so many times about offering myself as a living sacrifice, but now I'm beginning to understand experientially its life changing intent.

"Therefore, my brothers, I implore you by God's mercy to offer your very selves to Him: a living sacrifice, dedicated and fit for His acceptance, the worship offered by mind and heart. Adapt yourselves no longer to the pattern of this present world, but let your minds be remade and your whole nature thus transformed. Then you will be able to discern the will of God, and to know what is good, acceptable, and perfect."

Obviously, becoming a living sacrifice is a process, a daily commitment. I could feel myself incrementally modifying each judgmental, critical assessment of situations with more empathetic, patient visualizations of what scenarios could be. These modifications did not change the facts of adultery but did slowly change my behavior in relation to those facts. Slowly, ever so slowly, Sam's betrayal with his paramour released its grip on how I viewed myself. I realized that I was sacrificing my essence to the power Sam's lying infidelity had on me.

In this transitional state, I questioned God incessantly, each question, a trajectory, spiraling me on another series of thought tangents punctuated by scenes of mostly my trying to be vindicated. What a useless waste of emotional energy! It's so trite that it's embarrassing, the story told over and over again of the preacher who cheated on his wife! How do I resolve such a mess? I mean, aren't we, the ministers' wives, the ones most suited for the job of finding a scriptural answer to all of life's dilemmas?

My story is so typical of all those other wronged wives, the ones to whom I used to be so condescending in our marital security. I remember judgmentally saying, "How could they not possibly know that their husbands are unfaithful? Either their marriage is so pathetically un-intimate or they're lying! How can a minister stand in God's pulpit and preach knowing what he is doing?" How many times did I espouse these thoughts and proclaim them haughtily? I am ashamed to admit it and ask the forgiveness of the other preachers' wives whom I have condemned through the years. Who was the 'other woman' in my case?

Terry was a lovely, attractive, needy divorcee who had been struggling in an abusive marriage and here came my husband, the knight in shining armor who showed her tenderness, compassion, and understanding. I know all about it. That love had been mine. The only problem was that my receptacle of passion was used and familiar, one to be discarded. Sam no longer wanted me. He was ready for new flavors.

My thoughts kept returning to that pivotal painful date night. We had been to see the movie, '*The Horse Whisperer*' and in my cocoon of shared marital convictions, I was blabbering on at dinner in a local restaurant about how sick and tired I was of Hollywood glorified adultery.

"Couldn't we see a movie these days with a healthy romance instead of something perverted?" I was sharing my heartfelt reactions under the assumption we held in common certain moral standards. I was mistaken. His response stunned me.

Sam said something to the effect of, "I really appreciated how they acknowledged their mature feelings and realistically showed how married people can fall in love with someone else."

My head snapped up, and in his eyes, I recognized what he was saying. I retorted, "You're having an affair!"

Sam answered my statement with, "Let's go home." That's when I fell off my mountain and started frantically scrambling for some kind of footing. One year, one divorce, and his remarriage later, I'm still scrambling for a place to stand.

Another of the disheartening aspects of divorce besides the shattering of preconceived standards is that the habit of communicating with a significant other life's joys and sorrows is hard to forget. There comes a moment of sliding into a quick abyss upon realizing that when I'm glowing with the enthusiasm of some success or another, there is no immediate one with whom to share. I was in the final stages of earning my doctorate when I discovered my husband's adultery. My academic achievements and joy therein should have been a source of exuberance, yet I allowed Sam and his deceit to rob me of that. I came to realize that my self-worth was mine alone. I could not sacrifice it to Sam's view. Does that make sense? Instead of letting his opinion of my worth dictate who I was, I needed to intentionally take that power back! I kept praying and persevering, trying to say what Paul says in Philippians 4: 11–14.

"For I have learned to find resources in myself whatever my circumstances. I know what it is to be brought low, and I know what it is to have plenty. I have been very thoroughly initiated into the human lot with all its ups and downs, fullness and hunger, plenty and want. I have strength for anything through Him who gives me power." I am a living sacrifice. I am sacrificing my need to share life with a partner to God's acceptance of me.

I still have those desperate nights where the bottom of a pill bottle looks like an awfully attractive escape. Many nights, the only thing that keeps me alive is not wanting to add more pain to my boys. My friends say, "Look how you're blossoming," and my family says, "You're better off without him!" And some snatches of days, I cling to such altruism as well. But, the truth is, I was rejected. I was replaced. And I am alone.

Yes, I know about faith. Believe me, if it weren't for God's love, each day would be intolerable. But, today for some reason, I am compelled to talk about the pain. Tomorrow, I hope to be able to talk about the healing. Maybe the Psalmist is right after all when he says, "Tears may come at night fall, but joy comes in the morning."

In the night-time of pain, we feel like it's never going to end and specific happenings in our lives seem to validate the torture. About three months into this interminable prison of pain, Sam was out of the country for several weeks on a business trip with a couple of weeks added on for pleasure. Our denomination's world convention was in South Africa that year, one of Sam's favorite hunting destinations. He arranged flights for my boys to meet him after the convention for their own hunting trip. That cornered, allotted time away from Sam while he was out of the country was for me, a sentencing to contemplative hell. During this vacuum, I wrote and revamped endless lists comparing my assets to Terry's.

I would write and rewrite them, formulating a myriad of self-help agendas complete with triumphant results and imagined hoped for successes. For you see, Sam had informed me before he left that he was going to use this time to decide with whom he wanted to spend the rest of his life, me or Terry. He called me several times while away and the conversations were stiltedly distant and not only in miles. In one pivotal call, he said, "We (he and Terry) had our first fight and I panicked that she wouldn't want me anymore. I think that that is telling me that she's the one for me. I must beg for her forgiveness."

Let me remind you that I'm listening to this diatribe by phone without the advantage of body language and context. What rushed through my mind in a flush of heated awareness was that Terry's reaction was his primary concern. And more revealing than that was the fact that I couldn't remember Sam ever begging me for forgiveness about anything! Yet even with this illuminating humiliation, I was still desperately clinging to the chance that he would change his mind and come home to me.

In his absence, I buried myself in work and study. I was preparing for my imminent written doctoral finals and purposefully re-shifted mental energy towards my books and away from my shattered heart. Each day became a deliberate exercise in self-discipline monitored by rigorous scheduling and incessant prayer.

Listen to me, girls. Whatever you do that allows you to lose a sense of time and place can become your sanctuary for healing and an escape from pain. Allow yourself a vacation from pain by throwing yourself into a scheduled, regimented, planned activity that demands your utmost in mental or physical energies. Since I'm not athletic and don't enjoy the rigors of physical activity, my sanctuary is cerebral. I found that I could discipline my thoughts into a specific pursuit and subsequently discovered that time lapse eclipsed into a passion for knowing who I was through God's eyes. I no longer wanted to hide from God's scrutiny but relished His magnifying glass with a vengeance. Redirecting the energy I spent on self-loathing into energy spent on another activity of my choosing shed light on who I was in God's eyes instead of who I was in Sam's eyes.

I learned to say, "To know God is my one basic passion and purpose through my endeavors today." The pursuit of knowledge for me makes demands on the will as well as on the understanding. The pursuit of knowledge is an exciting curiosity. As well as God knows me, I want to know Him. "Examine me, O' God, and know my thoughts; test me and understand my misgivings. Watch lest I follow any path that grieves thee; Guide me in the ancient ways." (Psalm 139: 23–24)

When my finals were over, I woke up to the brutal dawn of anticipating Sam's return from his two-week trip abroad when he said he would make his decision about choosing me or Terry. I spent several days in preparation, fooling myself into believing that physical preparation would be a calling card, which he couldn't resist. I went through all the typical female grooming rituals of preparing for an exquisite date. I tried on several outfits and chose what I thought would be the perfect combination of feminine, alluring, yet understated attire.

I practiced tucking my red silk blouse in to show off my new trim waist or leaving it loose and soft to give just a hint of form underneath. My nails and hair were freshly done, and my skin glowed with eagerness. I had baked him coconut pie, his favorite, and had fixed another favorite dish, a chicken curry. All was set for the homecoming, which would swing my life in one direction or the other. "Please, God," I begged, "not the other way."

During these anticipatory preparations, I also had my boys in mind because they had met their dad on the last leg of his trip for a hunting expedition. I had requested Sam not to tell the boys of his affair until he had decided on his ultimate course of action. We could tell them together because I did not want them to experience devastation without my own reassuring comfort and presence. Unbeknownst to me, my wishes were not considered, and he told them anyway the night before they boarded the plane to come home. I cannot imagine the claustrophobic agony of digesting such a revelation within the confines of an airplane cabin! You wouldn't even have the luxury of private tears. I needed to wrap my arms around my boys, hold them close, and cushion the blows of betrayal.

To say that I was anxious driving to the airport to receive my family is certainly an understatement! Scanning the myriad faces disembarking from the overseas flights tightened the already clenched fist around my heart. The boys came off first. Their fierce hugs and whispered warnings of, "Not now, Mom," let me know immediately that they knew about the affair and they needed me to keep it together until we were safely within the confines of our car and home.

Sam was one of the last off the plane and his less-than-cursory glance spoke more than his lack of words. Yet, I still eagerly approached him, searching his face and grabbing for his arms. In return, I received nothing—no eye contact and no touch. To add to my spiraling devastating pain was the ensuing unfolding of events.

I don't enjoy driving, especially someplace new where I'm not sure of directions. I made it to the airport just fine and parked in one of those massive parking garages where each level is identical. One of my many inadequacies is a lack of a sense of direction, and added to my befuddled state of mind, it proved to be disastrous.

After meeting the flight and going through baggage claim, we headed to the car. But, I couldn't find the car anywhere! Sam berated me incessantly and in total defeat, I finally scrunched myself into an airport seat and succumbed again to the ever-present onslaught of tears. Sam was furious with me and this added disapproval felt like a cacophony of hammers haranguing my skull. Would the onslaught never quit? Finally, the airport security helped locate the car. It was one level over the spot that I had first indicated for its parking place. My older son ended up bundling me up in his embrace and coaxed me into the back seat of the car.

The ride home was horrible to say the least. My oldest son and Sam sat in the front while I huddled in the back. They yelled accusations and frustrations at each other most of the way home while I wept and intermittently interjected a pathetic plea that Sam reconsider and not leave us. The closer we got to home the more the car closed in on us. What a nightmare of a two-hour drive!

Of course, Sam's first item to be attended to on his arrival home was to call his Terry and plan an exuberant homecoming. I am ashamed and embarrassed to admit that even after all that rejection, I kept trying that evening. I attempted to allure him yet again and this time, he stopped me with, "Sheila, not again. Quit trying so hard. Leave it alone."

One reason I was trying so hard is that I was following our marriage counselor's instructions. He kept telling me to give him time to decide. However, the more that time passed, the faster Sam was slipping away from me. I could just imagine Terry glorying again in his presence, celebrating his return in triumph and helping him delegate me to the past. My time was running out, my husband was running to another, and my reserves were running on empty.

What can you do during those days when all hope has run dry and all you do is plod through one day just to be faced with another? I wish I had a list of all your names out there who have been through the same hopelessness. I could call you up and say, "OK...today you must get so and so done." Maybe our shared emptiness could become shared condolences, could become shared encouragement, and could become shared instructions.

We are to live our lives with intentionality, putting into action what we have experientially believed. Purposeful, intentional living gives us daily infusions of hope, dispelling some of the pain. How better to possess a sense of fulfillment than to be daily invigorated by a spiritual accomplishment laced into the routine of daily demands. Our pro-active lives become the definition of self-sacrifice. The sense of abandonment and loneliness after adultery becomes habitually replaced by a sense of fulfillment. My thought process becomes, *I am worthwhile because I am doing what God directed me to do today.*

"So, you too friends must be obedient as always; even more, now that I am away, than when I was with you. You must work out your own salvation in fear and trembling, for it is God who works in you, inspiring both the will and the deed, for his own chosen purpose." (Philippians 2: 12–13)

Anger

Chapter 3

Help, Lord, for loyalty is no more;
good faith between man and man is over.
One man lies to another:
they talk with smooth lip and double heart.
May the Lord make an end of such smooth lips,
and the tongue that talks so boastfully!
Psalm 12: 1–3

A huge struggle, and one about which I feel guilt, is my boys' relationship with their father. I know in my mind and even occasionally in my heart, that they need him. But, I get so angry that after he turned his back on them and walked away, he still gets to benefit from their love. Each time they talk or meet, jealousy rears its ugly head in a monstrous fashion. I hear Sam's voice on the phone's answering machine as he leaves messages for the boys and it turns my stomach. I want to lash out with venomous words, but I don't. It would benefit no one, especially the boys.

I'm learning to take the sudden blows like a pro! I purposefully extend my body to diffuse the jabs to the heart. The pain spreads thinner, gets weaker, and changes itself into debilitating anger directed at the other woman. The anger paralyzes me, and days later, I open my eyes to my little patch of world. The grass needs cutting desperately. The roses need tending, the paint is chipping on the eaves, and when I look up, I see that the branches of my huge oak tree are heavy with neglect. Wearily, I flop into the porch swing and give in to the loneliness, the horrid aloneness, that is my steady and faithful companion.

However, all days aren't played out in quite such an optimistic manner where I handle the blows of outrage and anger with grace. I woke up angry this morning, screaming that it wasn't my fault! Everyone is always saying, "It takes two to tango," and all those smug clichés about women who get dumped. But, why am I responsible for his adultery, for his abandoning me? Why do I worry so much about what others are concluding? Let them think what they will. I am secure in God's unwavering love for me and I will continue to stand on that foundation, for the next few hours anyway!

I nudge myself to remember what Paul said in Romans 8:31–39 and use those words for assurance and a road out of anger.

"With all this in mind, what are we to say? If God is on our side, who is against us? He did not spare his own Son, but gave him up for us all, and with this gift, how can he fail to lavish upon us all he has to give? Who will be the accuser of God's chosen ones? It is God who pronounces acquittal, then who can condemn? It is Christ—Christ who died, and more than that, was raised from the dead—who is at God's right hand, and indeed pleads our cause. Then what can separate us from the love of Christ? Can affliction or hardship? Can persecution, hunger, nakedness, peril, or the sword? For I am convinced that there is nothing in death or life, in the world as is or the world as it shall be, in the forces of the unwise, in heights or depths—nothing in all creation that can separate us from the love of God in Christ Jesus our Lord."

It has been difficult for me to write about my anger because I'm afraid that once the floodgates open, the torrent of primal rage will be out of control. Then I am filled with remorse and guilt for not being grateful and 'counting my blessings.' I must learn to be patient and quiet. But, don't you just hate it when people tell you that! They intend to use comforting words, but the words instead come across as fighting words.

It's hard to keep a smile plastered on my face when this happens because these people mean well, but it's like petting a porcupine—sharp and piercing. You know they're right, but knowing is not good enough to motivate me to follow through with the sound advice. In Psalms 37: 79, David, in all his failings, had to learn to: "wait quietly for the Lord and be patient till He comes; do not strive to outdo the successful nor envy him who gains his ends. Be angry no more, have done with wrath; strive not to outdo in evildoing. For evil doers will be destroyed, but they who hope in the Lord shall possess the land. A little while, and the wicked will be no more; look well, and you will find their place is empty."

I must recount the details of a time when my anger blind-sided me, and I was totally without boundaries. I must first give a little background information and set the stage.

As a missionary kid growing up outside the United States, I was not accustomed to the financial responsibilities that many children growing up here take for granted, because the opportunities for independence are interwoven in the American culture. For example, my first paying job was not until I was in college, likewise with a bank account. I didn't learn how to drive at sixteen, so I wasn't familiar with insurance procedures. Basically, I could travel the world, battle airport strikes, negotiate war zones, and talk my way out of predicaments in several languages. But driving or handling finances were not in my repertoire.

Therefore, it was easy and convenient to have Sam always handle all the finances and bills. I barely looked at phone bills, which in hindsight, probably helped facilitate Sam's adulterous affair. This was a huge fault on my part and one that I have regretted. For it has been a real struggle to learn the ins and outs of taxes, budgets, medical insurance, homeowner's policies, and other financial issues. Again, friends and family have stepped in to teach the forty-four-year-old novice the rules of the financial world.

I have been exceptionally proud of myself for coping and succeeding in this arena, especially navigating the intricacies of tax mazes. Consequently, I was quite appalled after tax season last year to receive a letter accompanying Sam's tax bill from the accountant stating that 'per our pre-arranged agreement' I was responsible for his bill. My reaction was immediate and volatile.

"Like hell I was!" This is from a man who had sent one miserly check to his boys the month he had left, and an occasional pittance here and there for spending money. The rationale was that I had kept the house and my student loan, and he had the debt from the credit cards. I accepted that agreement at the time of divorce and have fought to make ends meet each month on one salary. Getting that letter from the accountant sent me through the roof!

I had not been in the habit of calling Sam and his new family, because truthfully, I didn't want to hear Terry's voice. Just the voice had the power to ruin my outlook for days. Nevertheless, I jerked up the phone, pounded out their number, and was ready to do battle. As my luck would have it, Terry answered the phone with a cheerful, "Hello!"

I identified myself and asked to speak to Sam. She responded graciously by saying that he wasn't home, but anything that I wanted to say to him, I could say to her as well.

The floodgates opened, and I let it rip! No telling what all I said, but the gist of it was that I would appreciate it if he would pay his own bills and not send them to me, because I had not asked for any assistance in meeting medical payments for his children, which had been astronomical that year considering our severe and chronic medical issues. She reacted to my tirade with, "Sam always said that you were overemotional, so if you would calm down, maybe we could discuss this rationally."

The patronizing tone was like the match to a flint rock. No holds were barred now! I flew back at her in a rage with, "How dare you talk to me about emotions out of control! You of all people don't have a leg to stand on in the arena of out of control emotions. But, oh yeah, I forgot, that's not what you do with your legs. You spread yours for your preacher!"

God Almighty. Did all that filth come out of my mouth? It sure did and more as well! I was so absorbed in my righteous indignation that I didn't hear one of my sons walk in until he said, "What's going on? Who are you talking to?"

Startled out of my tunnel zone of anger, I capitulated into a puddle of tears. My son gently took the phone from me, spoke to Terry, and asked to have his dad call him later. Both sons spoke to him that night and it gave them the chance to voice their stance on some issues. I wasn't in on the conversation, but I did hear snatches from my perch on the couch. We, the three of us, were sitting together in the den toughing out the emotional aftermath of my explosion. One such morsel of overheard conversation included my son saying, "Fine, Dad. Why don't you just go ahead and have a good life with your new family!"

I was mortified and engulfed in shame to think that I had piled on my boys even more misery and heartache because of my angry reaction to a mere letter. Have you even guessed that your children's pain is even more severe than your own? That question hit me with needed enlightenment. I couldn't possibly know how hard it is on my boys. I'm not kin to my ex. I don't have his blood and his bones and his genes in me. How could he just walk away from his own? I would like to be enough for my children to fill their vacuum, but they too will have to learn that God's love is the only love pervasive enough to seep into all the nooks and crannies of a broken heart.

As Ephesians 3: 14–21 states, "With this in mind then, I kneel in prayer to the Father, from whom every family in heaven and on earth takes its name. That out of the treasures of his glory, he may grant you strength and power through his Spirit in your inner being, that through faith, Christ may dwell in your hearts in love. With deep roots and firm foundations, may you be strong to grasp, with all God's people, what is the breadth and length and height and depth of the love of Christ, and to know it, though it is beyond knowledge. So, may you attain to fullness of being, the fullness of God himself."

You are probably wondering now what became of that embarrassing demonstration of anger with Sam's new wife over the phone? Sam called me the next day and said that if I needed to talk to him, call him between eight and three in the day. I don't know about the time constraints, but I think it was so that I wouldn't call when she was at home so as to not antagonize and berate her again! I had stooped so low that I hardly recognized myself anymore. I had given Sam and Terry all the fuel and power they needed to justifiably say whatever they pleased about me. My anger was out of control.

Ask yourself the same question that I had to ask myself. In your flailing about, demanding people to see you as the victim, as the innocent party in this divorce, have you looked at yourself through Christ's piercing perceptive eyes? At first, I clung tenaciously to my ignorance, labeling it innocence. Next, I gift-wrapped this innocence, marked it righteousness, and presented it to my Lord. I was in for a rude awakening.

When I honestly and with full abandon see myself as I truly am, a sinner, just like Sam, saved by the awesome grace of God, then I can let go of my filthy sanctimonious righteousness, and continue healing. For isn't healing sanctification about becoming more like Christ every day? And isn't sanctification ongoing? I need to examine what my confession is and ask for a genuine clean heart, not one fabricated by my own false security of self-indulgent innocence.

I can't keep patching up my old feelings and expect them to apply to a new life. That was a turning point for me. It dawned on me that forgiveness does not mean forgetting. Anger is part of telling the truth about adultery. I warned myself not to bequeath anger the power and permission to control me. The apostle Luke wrote the forgiveness and forgetting story best in one of Jesus' parables. "He told them this parable also; no one tears a piece from a new cloak to patch an old one. If he does, he will have made a hole in the new cloak, and the patch from the new will not match the old. Nor does anyone put new wine into old wineskins; if he does, the new wine will burst the skins, the wine will be wasted, and the skins ruined. Fresh skins for new wine! (A fresh perspective for a new life) And no one after drinking old wine wants new; for he says, 'the old wine is good.'" (Luke 5: 36–39)

To ease my conscience, I wrote Sam and Terry both a letter of apology, aired some concerns, and promised not to interrupt their lives again unless it concerned the boys. So far, I've stuck to that and I pray that that sort of venomous rage doesn't take over me again.

In your experience as a divorced Christian woman, do you find that a crisis will magnify whether or not you have been practicing listening to the Holy Spirit's inclinations within you? Have you allowed God to build your character so that a crisis becomes a challenge instead of a debilitating monstrosity? Not only is our salvation a constant reason for rejoicing, but it is also the consistent fuel for striving. Salvation is a gift of strength and courage draped in vigilant holiness. God does not shield us from the requirements of adoption, but our familial likeness to Jesus Christ through the indwelling Holy Spirit makes us equipped, not spoiled, decisive, not pampered, and courageous, not weak.

I can rant and rave, and conjure up all manners of despicable torture to befall Sam and his new wife in my own lapses into imagined vengeance. But I have no right to inflict that type of poison on another in reality. Hopefully, those lapses will become less and less, and I won't care so much anymore.

I can agree with the Old Testament Prophet Jeremiah when he was so worried about vengeance. "But the Lord is on my side, strong and ruthless. Therefore, my persecutors shall stumble and fall powerless. Bitter shall be their abasement when they fail, and their shame shall long be remembered. The Lord of Hosts, thou dost test the righteous and search the depths of the heart; to thee have I committed my cause, let me see thee take vengeance on them. Sing to the Lord, praise the Lord; for he rescues the poor from those who would do them wrong." (Jeremiah 20: 11–13)

The fire of anger burns so hot inside my gut that it even scares me sometimes. Leave vengeance to the Lord! Experience the truth and vulnerability of a healthy anger as an authentic emotion, not a controlling arbiter of your well-being.

Fear
Chapter 4

Cease to dwell on days gone by
and to brood over past history.
Here and now, I will do a new thing;
this moment, it will break from the bud.
Can you not perceive it?
I will make a way even through the wilderness
and paths in the barren desert;
Isaiah 43:18–19

Will I ever have a future without trembling hesitant fear? Why do I constantly cover up my fear, wanting others to see me not only as a managing survivor, but a confident striver? After being very ill this year with hepatitis and then having to have gallbladder surgery, my body was absorbing all the pain. People are right when they say, "A broken heart makes a broken body." I became afraid of contact with people and wanted to hide. I was petrified with fear of what else life was going to bring my way.

Slowly, with the constant support of family and friends, I am emerging with hesitant confidence that there is life as a single person. I have finished my doctorate this year, I have kept my home, I have published several articles, and I'm starting to write a book. On those days, I can push fear aside and stomp it down.

The fear factor can leak into other relationships, especially those that are beyond the surface level. If every effect must have an adequate cause, then the effect of trust is the honest heart to heart, mind to mind, soul to soul connection, not only between me and my Lord, but between me and others giving me purpose, meaning, and fulfillment. That is the kind of relationship I mistakenly thought I had in my marriage, so I'm afraid to venture out and circulate again. Dating—what an appealing but ghastly thought! I've gone out some—a few pleasant, but others disastrous! The fear of rejection can be stifling. Some days, I find confidence through my trust in God that no amount of discouragement or loneliness can destroy, even when I waiver. I pray that my boys can trust in my love for them in the same way.

I don't want to reach a season in my journey where a life of horrifying lovelessness frightens me to the point of numbing detachment from others. It's temptingly safe, but way too sad. Self-pity follows fear. It bites at it heals. I say to myself, "Go away, fear. Leave me alone!"

Instead, wouldn't it be great if we could change our perspective like changing sleep sides at night? Flop over one way and be lonely, flop over the other way and loneliness is blessed solitude. I want to be determined to change the loneliness of solitude into a precious gift of pure joy and introspection. My desire is to take advantage of this time of being alone and not be afraid.

When I wake up at night and can't go back to sleep, maybe then the Lord can speak to me in His special way with not only words of comfort, but words of insight and illumination. Introspection can be good and cleansing, giving redirection and focus to the issues that first woke us up from our slumber. When we hear the Lord speaking during these quiet moments, the terrors of fear are not so severe anymore.

"Thou, Lord, my allotted portion, thou my cup, thou dost enlarge my boundaries. The lines fall for me in pleasant places; indeed, I am well content (almost) with my it\ inheritance (of divorce). I will bless the Lord who has given me counsel; in the nighttime, wisdom comes to me in my inward parts. I have set the Lord continually before me: with him at my right hand, I cannot be shaken. Therefore, my heart exults, and my spirit rejoices, my body too rests unafraid." (Psalms 16: 5–9)

Fear brought a terrifyingly close call for me one night, as I sped away from being with Sam at a hotel and dinner where we were meeting as part of our University's faculty. Sam had previously planned to meet Terry after the scheduled meetings were over, extending his time at the resort for another night. I was driving home on a lonely dark stretch of country road, my eyes blinded by tears knowing what I had left behind. I wished for a crash, blessed nothingness without feeling.

I sensed my foot pressing hard on the pedal. I didn't even try to ease up. Yet, I wasn't brave enough to go the whole way. I laughed while smearing the tears off my face. "You're too scared to go on without him and you're too scared to end life because of him. How pathetic can you get," my thoughts screamed at me. I felt suspended, entombed in my imagination, seeing his grief and guilt when he was finally told that I was gone. "Oh yeah! He doesn't care if you are gone or not…remember?" But, I was still alive. Scared, I drove on. I just wanted to be home.

Have you noticed how divorce strips you down to nothing? Not only are you naked and exposed before your maker, but before your family, friends, and yourself. All the props are yanked away. At first, you're trying to regain your balance, then you glance down and are shocked to see the raw nakedness. I have been reduced to simply 'me.' I am no longer what my friends think of me or what I used to think of myself dressed in my varying job descriptions of minister's wife, teacher, home-maker, and mom.

I ask myself, "Now, naked as I am, am I willing to hand myself over to God?" If so, He can clothe me with His righteousness and my life can be free of my own futile cravings and instead be persistently steadfast in knowing Him. The joy of my salvation has been renewed! At least, it has been renewed for a few days. My prayer becomes like the Psalmist in 51: 10–12, "Create a pure heart in me, O God, and give me a new and steadfast spirit. Do not drive me from thy presence or take thy Holy Spirit from me. Revive in me the joy of thy deliverance and grant me a willing spirit to uphold me."

Every now and then, I do have those days that are jumbled with fear and agitation. Is calm and peace what I am looking for? But, if calm and peace mean the absence of passion, then forget it. I can't deny my core. I think that peace without passion would be like silence—pleasing and soothing for a spell, but in the unraveling of a calm spell, my feelings would leak out anyway. I'm reminded again of one of the main things about me that used to irk Sam. I did express myself boisterously with a lot of feeling. Sam would say to me, "Don't laugh so loud, don't get so excited, keep your voice down, and don't be so emotional." Yet, when I responded with passion to him and we were alone in moments of intimacy, he never complained!

Wouldn't it be a refreshing relief to jump off the emotional treadmill? However, one advantage of running the course after divorce is that I have had to depend on the Lord for keeping me going. Yet, I ask myself, "Am I using God for just self-actualization in times of need, or am I truly seeking Him?" Ask yourself that question. While we are being tested in the divorce times of injustice, humiliation, rejection, and ingratitude are we using prayer and scripture only as a peaceful respite from the pain? Instead, I want to focus on knowing Him and not merely experiencing some of the benefits of being his child. Truly desiring God is equivalent to truly desiring a new vulnerable life not controlled by fear. I can almost concur with the author of Philippians. At least ideally, I would love to be able to say that I do.

"All I care for is to know Christ, to experience the power of his resurrection, and to share his sufferings, in growing conformity with his death, if only I may finally arrive at the resurrection from the dead. It is not to be thought that I have already achieved all this. I have not yet reached perfection, but I press on, hoping to take hold of that for which Christ once took hold of me. My friends, I do not reckon myself to have got hold of it yet. All I can say is this; forgetting what is behind me, and reaching out for that which lies ahead, I press towards the goal to win the prize which is God's call to the life above in Christ Jesus." (Philippians 3:10–12)

I crave being alone, yet, at the same time, I fear it. It's not that I don't enjoy having time to myself. That's not it at all. I relish getting so engrossed in a book that time is lost. Wandering around a mall or discovering new shops on my own is a special treat. Digging in the dirt, cultivating a garden, only hearing nature's voices, is immensely satisfying. Waking up early while the rest of the world is still asleep and spending time rediscovering a favorite passage of scripture with just my cat staring at me is my ideal style for starting a day.

I even enjoy going out to eat by myself. I choose a restaurant with comfortable booths and good lighting, meticulously select an engrossing book to read, allot myself a couple of hours of nursing a drink and nibbling on finger food, and wile away the time encircled by buzzing conversations and bursts of laughter. These kinds of alone times are a gift; vignettes of my choosing that are void of fear.

Ask yourself this, "Are you living out of fear or freedom?" Some days what dominates my thinking is the fear of growing old alone. Maybe I need to alter that thinking to one of freedom to grow old single. Helping my aging parents lately and watching my mother's devotion as she takes care of my father who has Alzheimer's has emotionally brought me to my knees. Doesn't that kind of love, care, and tenderness come from a lifetime of intimacy in marriage? I can't imagine someone taking care of me that way unless cushioned and fortified with a volume of shared memories. As each page is turned in the shared scrapbook of experiences, new strength is gleaned just from the sheer enormity of love's commitment. Again, that fear of being old alone envelopes me with full force, and I need to give it up.

From being afraid of growing old single to being afraid not to have anyone with whom to share life's joys, divorce robs us of the security of approaching each day with eagerness. Being truly alone is not having anyone with whom to wait out a grandchild being born. Divorce interrupts the continuity of life and negates the shared joy of anticipating those grandchildren. And sleeping alone…how about that one insignificant fact in the whole scheme of divorce? Do you have as much trouble with that as I do? I am learning to sleep alone. I know it doesn't sound like much, but to me, it is momentous! Sometimes, I go all night without thinking about the man who used to sleep with me. The ache is still there.

I'm learning to live alone with gratitude and some limited thanksgiving. I try not to regret as much, but instead, find myself looking forward to the possibilities that might lie ahead. Again and again, I turn to the Psalms for soothing comfort, knowing that a myriad of people before me have felt the same fear of loneliness. "God is our shelter and our refuge, a timely help in trouble. So, we are not afraid when the earth heaves and the mountains are hurled into the sea, when its waters seethe in tumult and the mountains quake before his majesty. There is a river whose streams gladden the city of God, which the Most High has made his holy dwelling. God is in that city; she will not be overthrown, and He will help her at the break of day." (Psalms 46: 1–5)

What about weddings? I'm afraid of my boys' weddings. They had so looked forward to their father not only marrying them but being the Grande Chef at the cook-out for the rehearsal dinners. Sam and I used to plan for these future occasions with fondness and talk about the what-ifs together. Those daydreams are now up in smoke, burned by the fires of his lust.

Sometimes, the feelings of regret and aloneness are so poignant that I am violently swept by a fierce longing for love and intimacy. Before I can wrestle it down once again, it has me pinned down. Wouldn't it be a relief to be free of this desire for shared trusts, confidences, and dreams? If I hadn't experienced this bond before, I wouldn't miss it so much now. Instead of fond memories of a bond, it has become an aching bondage of need. I try sublimating this need with reassurance of God's provision in all our needs, but it's hard. Some days, I am grateful to be free of the obligation of meeting another's needs. And then, I vacillate and crave the sense of being needed. How can Christ handle this dilemma? He created me and knows each and every nuance of my configurations; therefore, He also knows the solutions to each and every challenge of a broken fearful heart.

"Weak men we may be, but it is not as such that we fight our battles. The weapons we wield are not merely human, but divinely potent to demolish strongholds. We demolish sophistries and all that rears its proud head against the knowledge of God. We compel every human thought to surrender in obedience to Christ; and we are prepared to punish all rebellion when once you have put yourselves in our hands. Look facts in the face." (2 Corinthians 10: 3–6)

As pastor and wife, Sam and I used to grudgingly officiate at weddings where the bride and grooms' families were split by divorce. Our comments to each other at such occasions were ones of thanksgiving that our boys wouldn't have to go through that kind of nonsense and discomfort of which spouse belongs to whom and who is speaking to whom. And now, I have that to look forward to. I add another fear on the calculator of divorce. Yet, I must remember that the choice in letting go of the notion that I'm in this alone is mine to make. A heightened awareness of life's riches rinse through me, cleansing me somehow. Fear is pushed aside again for a bit.

How can I appeal to you women out there who are going through the same fears? Let me reassure you that life is not a series of oddities and extemporaneous ironies strung together haphazardly. Even this divorce, as off-kilter as it is, must fit into the puzzle of my life somehow and I must stop stubbornly refusing to let the pieces be placed on the cushioned surface of the card table. Maybe the jagged edges and misshapen corner pieces of the puzzle will someday be crucial pieces without which the pleasant scene of future experiences can't be complete. I must trust in God's omniscience and omnipotence to remake me out of the strewn pieces of divorce. Maybe it's not too late to wonder what we are going to be when we grow up!

"When I was a child, my speech, my outlook, and my thoughts were all childish. When I grew up, I had finished with childish things. Now we see only puzzling reflections in a mirror, but then we shall see face to face. My knowledge is now partial, then it will be whole like God's knowledge of me. In a word, there are three things that last forever: faith, hope, and love. But the greatest of them all is love." (1 Corinthians 13: 11–13)

I absolutely must get over the fear of not being safe. As a minister's wife, I felt securely protected within the confines of the church. My expectations, duties, and even challenges were clear. Now my responsibility is to redefine who I am outside the minister's wife parentheses.

After two years, the circumstances of my spouse's leaving still prick me and draw blood, but they aren't fatal wounds. I know that now. I am no longer living under Sam's unloving tutelage. I don't have to be afraid anymore of his disapproval. His disapproval felt like an athlete's stiff-armed block. I saw this abusive pattern in pursed lips or a quiet shunning withdrawal.

I can remember this pattern playing out at social gatherings: laughing, talking, boisterously interacting, and then glancing over to see Sam discreetly signaling me to tone it down. During a moment of joy, I was censored. This editing censorship made me constantly leery of outside relationships. I felt like I had to first ask permission, then seek incremental validation from Sam in social interactions to remain within the parameters of his approval. This continuous emotional refereeing was exhausting and self-eroding. Never more evident was this pattern than in the safety bubble of a church congregation!

In each successive assignment or congregation, Sam would seek out pastoral counseling situations where women would lay bare their souls. He was addicted to those cozy relationships where the exhilarating flirtatiousness of shared confidences took place. Sam was adept at the orchestrating of transfers to yet another job and another location so as not to face the consequences of deepening relationships with these women. We never stayed at a church for more than three years.

I learned to be quite verbally skilled at justifying each move for the general public. Each shift, I followed willingly and with enthusiasm, always looking forward to that honeymoon period with a new congregation and a new assignment. Now, with hindsight, I feel pretty sure that those moves had to do with women. It was easier to move than to deal with relationships that crossed the line. It was easier for him to be 'called' to another church, another assignment, than face the outcomes of his affairs. A move facilitated endings. I see that pattern clearly now.

I can look back and see different women, all discontent in their marriages: another missionary's wife, a deacon's wife, an estranged wife, all good women seeking guidance and solace from the kind and listening preacher. I can even remember walking up to one woman after church as she hung on his arm and looked adoringly into his eyes. I gently but firmly removed her hand and said, "This is my husband." I later learned that she continued to write to him, asking for career advice and direction after we had moved on from that church. I learned of these women from Sam himself. He told me these stories when I confronted him with my suspicions during the final unraveling of our marriage. He showed no remorse or shame, just acceptance of the facts.

These episodes of infidelity haunt me. Instead of phrases and words knifing into my thoughts, I want to not be afraid of my own memories in my own home. My home needs to be my safe refuge for calmer thoughts where anxiety no longer rules. I'm tired of having to apologize for or sublimate my personality and intelligence. I take three steps forward in confident passion and two steps back in quaking self-esteem. Others tell me that I've shown stamina and resilience during this time of divorce, but I'm tired and want some loving arms around me.

Not only am I plagued with fearful memories of Sam's affairs, but I'm also afraid of the dating life. I don't know the rules of that game. I don't want to fall back into old patterns of degrading self-thoughts and doubts that choke out my passion for life. I don't want to feel guilty anymore that I could have done more to save my marriage. I have tasted the pleasure of being proud of myself, of being an authentic person who is no longer preoccupied with justifying another's existence.

I pray that that sense of worth and pleasure in myself can carry past the characterization of the ex-minister's wife. I want to feel alive and vital, and sort of reaching out, running in my mind toward something, feeling things so strongly that in confidence and assurance, I'm stretching towards good times that are bound to lie ahead. I have a growing sense of belonging to the living world at large and not just that dark and sad portion when I'm with my memories of sharply defined alienation. Belonging to the living world means that I have to let the Lord wipe away my tears and no longer worry about the consequences of Sam's actions.

"He will wipe every tear from their eyes; there shall be an end to death and to mourning and crying and pain. For the old order has passed away! Then he who sat on the throne said, 'Behold! I am making all things new!' (And he said to me, 'Write this down; for these words are trustworthy and true. Indeed, they are already fulfilled.') I am the Alpha and the Omega, the beginning and the end. A draught from the water-springs of life will be my free gift to the thirsty. All this is the victor's heritage; and I will be his God and he shall be my son. But as for the cowardly, the faithless, and the vile, murderers, fornicators, sorcerers, idolaters, and liars of every kind, their lot will be the second death, in the lake that burns with sulfurous flames."

Being an active, present participant in life needed to replace the odd sense of detachment as an observer, which occupied so much of my languid time. It's comfortable, yet not comforting that way. For example, I felt like I was watching a play my first Christmas and Thanksgiving as a divorced woman. Frantically, the calls and pleas went out to family members that "Sheila is in desperate need." That Thanksgiving, we all gathered at my sister's home, all five of us: siblings, spouses, children, children's spouses, and our one new and precious great grandchild. I felt like I was on the fringe, outside looking in on the family gathering, not a participant, but as an attendee.

It's funny looking back on it how desperately I needed family, affirmation, stability, and security. I wanted to be strong enough to receive the love that I was demanding of them. During those holidays, my only safety was a vantage point, not of aloofness, but a separateness, looking on from the outskirts of the family circle. It reminded me of dodge ball as a kid at recess. I never was that quick or agile, so staying on the periphery, not exposing myself to the stinging blows shot from the encircling participants was safest. And then, I would keep my ear cocked for the recess bell so that I could escape to the successes of the classroom. I wanted to jump into my family circle, to be a participant, but I didn't have the strength.

I wanted family members to ask me how I was, but I dreaded their queries. I needed their compassionate hugs but cringed under their sympathies. After lunch, when different ones were settling in for comfortable conversation, relaxed TV watching, and mindless game playing, I pleaded exhaustion, spread a blanket on the grass, and pretended napping. I listened to the soothing hum of my sisters' conversations there on the back porch. Their family reminiscences and remembrances unintentionally pricked my festering divorce wound. I was afraid of being all in with my own family! Nevertheless, I was starting to feel myself healing. At least there a scab over that wound of divorce. Fear of being completely myself, of being insecurely not married anymore was no longer bleeding out. The flow of fear was being staunched by the love of my family and friends.

Trust

Chapter 5

I am my beloved's,
his longing is all for me.
Come, my beloved, let us go out into the fields
to lie among the henna-bushes.
Let us go early to the vineyards
and see if the vine has budded or its blossom opened,
if the pomegranates are in flower.
There will I give my love,
when the mandrakes give their perfume,
and all rare fruits are ready at our door,
fruits new and old,
which I have in store for you, my love.
Song of Songs 7: 10–13

At one point, at one juncture, I was adamantly positive that I would never trust again, a man that is. It's a disease and a sickness and God is tenderly healing me with assurance and steadfast nurturing.

Though desperately lonely and craving to be cherished, I know without a doubt who I am and that I'm called out by my name. Just like Jesus called to Mary by her name and broke through her grief in the Garden after His death, so our Father calls us to Him by name during our darkest times. We are called by our names so that we can recognize who is calling us. We can look up through our tears and confusion and recognize the face of care and love. "Have no fear. For I have paid your ransom; I have called you by name and you are my own. When you pass through deep waters, I am with you. When you pass through rivers, they will not sweep you away. Walk through fire and you will not be scorched, through flames and they will not burn you. For I am the Lord, your God, the Holy One of Israel, your deliverer." (Isaiah 43: 1–2) Now, dear sisters, there is a promise on which I can depend!

Nevertheless, the fact remains that I miss shared trusts. Odd, how intensely you knew a person, or thought you did, when you were drenched and soaked in love—only to discover later that perhaps you didn't know that person quite as well as you had imagined. Or more to the painful center, weren't quite as well-known as you had hoped, to have word and gesture cherished unconditionally. Thankfully, that is how God knows us.

In fact, He knows us so well that even when we don't feel like talking to Him, our dissatisfaction is enough for Him to hear. Take comfort in His knowledge of you! For me, even this is worship, knowing that I can throw anything at God as long as I'm communicating and recognize His presence. Remember Psalm 139 and keep it close to your heart to pull out when the grief blurs a bleak landscape.

"Lord thou has examined me and knowest me. Thou knowest all, whether I sit down or rise up, thou hast discerned my thoughts from afar. Thou hast traced my journey and my resting places, and art familiar with all my paths. For there is not a word on my tongue, but thou knowest them all. Thou hast kept close guard before me and behind and hast spread thy hand over me. Such knowledge is beyond my understanding, so high that I cannot reach it." (Psalm 139)

Do you ever think about the impossibility of ever knowing another partner, about the frailty of the constructs people make? I muse like an artist—vignettes and tableaus of memories—are they to be repainted, recast? Or do they still envelop, like soft packing wool, wrapped in their own legacy? Do they have the power to have their own legacy even if one of the characters abdicated? All our memories are woven into our life's tapestry and we cannot arbitrarily cut them out. We learn from our mistakes and our successes and continue to help ourselves and our families to grow out of the pain of divorce. But, aren't you sick and tired of all these lessons of life? I am!

"For everything, it's season and for every activity under heaven, it's time; a time to be born and a time to die, a time to plant and a time to uproot, a time to kill and a time to heal, a time to pull down and a time to build up, a time to weep and a time to laugh, a time for mourning and a time to gather them, a time to embrace and a time to refrain from embracing, a time to seek and a time to lose, a time to keep and a time to throw away, a time to tear down and a time to mend, a time for silence and a time for speech, a time to love and a time to hate, a time for war and a time for peace." (Ecclesiastes 3: 1–8)

In trying to regain a trusting footing, I frame and re-frame pictures of my boys, trying to capture finite moments of feeling to reassure myself. My children are my legacy. May I never disappoint them as a mother. I had to finally wake up from the dormancy of silence after divorce to take care of them. For at first, that was the only motivation to go on. During the darkest days of the aftermath of divorce, when my arms felt like dead weight and I could not make myself rise in the morning, the thought of causing more pain by not being there for my children became motivation to get moving again.

Our children are our gifts from God, entrusted to us for care and nurturing. Maybe I had messed up as a wife and fallen short of that job description, but I did know how to love my children. That was a lifelong job of which I refused to let go. I was reminded of the parental instructions of Proverbs 1: 7–9: "Attend my son to your father's instruction and do not reject the teaching of your mother. For they are a garland of grace on your head and a chain of honor around your neck."

I knew all along after the divorce that my husband was going to marry again. At one point after he had left home and before the divorce was final, he called me and asked me to reconsider our relationship. He apologized for the pain that he had caused, but he said he did not regret the affair. He said he couldn't promise that he wouldn't see Terry anymore and that he wanted to continue to keep up with how her girls were doing. Sam reinforced that he didn't want to break any promises to Terry's girls since they had been so abused by their father. He didn't think that they could handle any more disappointment. The only way that I would try our marriage again was if he promised never to see her, speak to her, write her, or contact her in any way.

It would not have been logistically difficult, since she lived two hours away, but he said he could never agree to that. I knew what a struggle it would be to repair the betrayed trust in the best of circumstances, but with the additional factor of continued contact, mending the shredded trust would not be possible. He had thrown the preciousness of marital intimacy in my face by sharing himself with another.

What is intimacy anyway? Intimacy is one of the basic needs with which we are all born. However, without complete and unadulterated honesty, you cheat yourself of the full meat of intimacy. We have the perfect example in what Christ offers us. Intimacy with Christ is coming to each other; he reaches out to me and I respond, without exterior interference. Intimate love never waivers and accepts unconditionally, just as we are. I don't have to be perfect first before searching for an intimate relationship with Christ. Intellectual intimacy—persistent Bible study—takes the gnarled complications of life and transforms them into directions and signposts. And I urgently needed direction!

"We ask God that you may receive from Him all wisdom and spiritual understanding for full insight into His will, so that your manner of life may be worthy of the Lord and entirely pleasing to Him. We pray that you may bear fruit in active goodness of every kind and grow in the knowledge of God. May he strengthen you in His glorious might, with ample power to meet whatever comes with fortitude, patience, and joy; and to give thanks to the Father who has made you fit to share the heritage of God's people in the realm of light." (Colossians 1: 9–12)

I had grown so accustomed to measuring my worth by Sam's opinions that I had lost the ability to trust my own decision-making process. My inner conversation insisted on baby steps. So, I ventured out of my stagnant mindset of victimhood. It was time to be decisive on my part. I started by taking my maiden name back when I knew that he was marrying Terry. I first consulted my boys and they supported my desire for a name change as they had supported me throughout the continuing ordeal.

Out of financial necessity, we revamped our lifestyle, since credit card bills had stacked up because of Sam's secret bank accounts and my not paying attention to bills. We were dependent on my salary alone. Sam never even offered to help. He stated that the boys were eighteen and considered adults by law, so he didn't have to support us in any way. So, we regrouped, and they moved back home to finish their university schooling. Home was our house designated for University faculty only and located on the edge of campus. Fortunately, we were benefiting from tuition remission since I worked at their university. My family and friends pitched in, and we made it through the first year.

I had expected some assistance from his parents for their grandchildren, but that was not to be either. Medical bills have been a real problem. One of my sons and I, both have chronic illnesses and I had to have emergency surgery on my pancreas and gall bladder in all this chaos. I had to tell the various agencies that I could pay so much each month and that was it. Financial strain is one of those ripple effects of divorce that isn't considered during the first emotional agonies. The nuts and bolts of living must be dealt with and I learned to swallow my pride and ask for help. I also learned very quickly that some people tie strings to their assistance. It can be emotional blackmail that during the strains of divorce is not needed.

I followed my mother's sage advice, and poured myself into my students' lives during the day and attended to my boys' needs in the evenings. My children started to hang out at home more often, bringing their friends with them. I remember on one occasion; my oldest son prepared a home-cooked gourmet meal for his girlfriend to celebrate a special occasion instead of taking her out. We found all kinds of ways to cut corners to save money. Many times, their fraternity brothers would come to the house just because! I so enjoyed throwing together impromptu meals and soaking in their boisterous presence. Generosity with my children came easily, but with other relationships, not so much.

Have you found it taxing to be generous again? A hard thing for me to do when in pain is to give of myself. The reserves were depleted, materially and emotionally. Yet, I experienced that if I purposefully and with diligence found even a minuscule way to give each day, then that day became worth living just to share in the joy on the receiver's face. Professionally, I was a college professor and counselor, so giving was part of the DNA of the job. Nevertheless, to continue to develop trust, I had to re-learn to give. I needed to stop acting like a helpless victim and get out of myself. If I concentrated on finding ways to tangibly give each day instead of concentrating on fantasies of revenge, I could see my steps towards healing and trusting again.

I encourage you to try not to: "Outdo the evildoers who emulate those who do wrong. For like grass, they soon wither and fade like the green of spring. Trust in the Lord and do good; settle in the land and find safe pasture. Depend upon the Lord, and he will grant you your heart's desire. Commit your life to the Lord; trust in Him and He will act. He will make your righteousness shine clear as the day and the justice of your cause like the sun at noon. Wait quietly for the Lord, be patient till He comes." (Psalms 37: 1–6)

Nevertheless, sometimes when working on self-trust, you can get de-railed. Fortunately, I have a good job, a supportive work atmosphere, and colleagues that respect my work.

An example of derailment happened during the first year of divorce. I was in the final phases of working on my doctorate and dissertation. One horrendous day, the last day of my comprehensive finals, I was in an isolated room plowing through the last of the four-day written exams when the mobile phone rang in my purse. The phone was Sam's and I had it while he was out of the country for a University-sponsored trip. I picked it up to answer and it was Terry, the 'other woman.' The ensuing conversation need not be reported, but suffice it to say, my performance on that test came to a screeching halt. I don't remember what I said to Terry, but I'm sure I let her have it.

After hanging up, I discovered on the phone all the stored messages from her to Sam and tortured myself again as I listened to her 'sweet nothings!' Remember that at this time, Sam had been gone on his trip for several weeks. Terry was in the habit, apparently, of phoning him daily to leave endearing messages as a countdown of how many days till she got to see him again. I don't know why I brought the phone with me that day, since I normally hated being tied to a phone and used it only in emergencies. How was I going to finish my final? How could I get my head together and refocus?

Fortunately, my habit was to outline in detail my answers before writing a final draft. I had already completed three fourths of my test responses and the remaining were still clearly outlined. I shut down, gathered up my things, and ran out of the examination. My gracious professor accepted the abbreviated outline format and I escaped that pressure-filled keg of the solitary examination room. Thankfully, my professors were quite understanding since they were already appraised of my circumstances and my outlines were detailed and adequately showed my proficiency on the subjects being tested. What a harrowing draining day that was!

Derailment incidents that annihilated trust did not decrease on Sam's return to the country. As I was unpacking his bag, a normal expected duty of mine, I noticed a large manila envelope. I opened it. To my horror, there spilled before me a whole roll of pictures of Terry in a motel room (I recognized the tell-tale generic furniture) and a slew of love letters. Sam had taken these mementos with him on his out of the country trip as a keepsake and reminder of their 'love.' Any resemblance of trust was obliterated with that discovery! As I re-live that moment of clarity and discovery a couple of years later, the nausea still overwhelms me as I remember that numbing pain of undeniable betrayal. If I had harbored any doubts before, I couldn't anymore.

Trust had been wiped out. I felt totally disconnected from Sam. Connectedness and family, relationships and commitment, these are not possible without the essential ingredient of trust. When Sam walked out on us with his infidelity, that connectedness was forcefully snipped like razor sharp shears through a strand of hair.

Are you ever adamantly positive that you will never be able to trust again? Doesn't it feel like a disease, a sickness in which you need nurturing and healing? Trust me on this. Healing is available, but it comes in pieces. How? As I approach my heavenly Father with confidence, laying out this fear to trust again, I am secure in His loving response and can learn to navigate the journey towards renewed hope in trust.

"Since therefore, we have a great high priest who has passed through the heavens, Jesus, the Son of God, let us hold fast to the religion we profess. For ours is not a high priest unable to sympathize with our weaknesses, but one who, because of his likeness to us, has been tested every way, only without sin. Let us, therefore, boldly approach the throne of our gracious God, where we may receive mercy and in His grace, find timely help." (Hebrews 4: 14–16)

I was tired of betrayals, of lies, of deceit. When I confronted Sam about the letters and pictures, he turned it around and belligerently accused me of invading his privacy. Even though he expected me to always pack and unpack his bags, I had dared to open an unmarked sealed envelope.

How did I respond? I relapsed and did what I habitually had done in the past. I cowered under this turnaround of blame.

I gazed through a film of tears into the eyes of the man I had loved, into the eyes of my betrayer. The man who was my husband, on whom I had always counted, my best friend, was now a stranger. He knew me so well that he also knew how to hurt me better than anyone else. I was confused and humiliated. I could no longer believe in him. Trust is the gift we give each other in marriage. I was found wanting again. His position or stance was that he did not do wrong by taking pictures of his lover in a motel room. I had done wrong by invading his privacy and finding those pictures.

Nothing devastates self-esteem like betrayal. Whatever descriptors are used to explain away betrayal doesn't really matter. Because the reality is that the betrayed partner in adultery is viewed as not only lacking, but not worthy of honesty, cheapened. I am just beginning to learn that Sam, the adulterer, was not worthy of my gift of trust. Integrity had disappeared from his life.

What is Integrity? Integrity is in part knowing God and then reflecting that knowledge in one's thoughts and actions. A definition of integrity for me is living out the absolutes of God's law in the reality of life. The world promotes random relativity as the caring option for successful relationships. But reckless relativity can be dangerous. It can shipwreck a life because of a skewed compass.

With Christ's thoughts being our thoughts, we can navigate through the vagaries of life with directional, purposeful, proactive confidence, having the likeness of Christ as our beacon. How does God's word instruct us in the development of integrity? In Philippians 4: 8–9, the instruction states, "and now my friends, all that is true, all that is noble, all that is just and pure, all that is lovable and gracious, whatever is excellent and admirable—fill all your thoughts with these things. The lessons I taught you, the tradition I have passed on, all that you heard me say or saw me do, put into practice, and the God of peace will be with you."

Trust after adultery is not an issue only between spouses. As one of my sons put it, "Dad, you don't get it. It's not just between you and Mom. When you dump on Mom, you dump on us too." The father whom the boys had trusted and on whom they counted was yanked away. Their father had been their hero. Now what? My oldest son was like a caged animal, roaring, growling, and lashing out. This was never directed at me, but at the world at large. Thankfully, he played football. I was so grateful for legal violence! I pitied the poor teammates that he pummeled every day in practice, beating out his anger and frustration.

My youngest son internalized the pain. He would practice his advice to me, which was, "Mom, don't think about him. Put him out of your mind. That's what I do." That son had always been the life of the party, the one with the quick wit. Months passed without my seeing his humor. Betrayal and broken promises drown the whole family, not just the broken couple. For if you can't count on Dad, who is a preacher, keeping his promises, who can you trust? I can just hear our boys searching. "How can you go back on everything you taught us and believe and—and then don't believe suddenly because 'you can't help how you feel?'" That's exactly what they asked him.

Not only does shattered trust erode our family relationships, but the ripple effects of severed trust lapped into all the congregations where we had pastored as well. I received calls and letters of support, but also calls and letters of enlightenment, telling me of other women, of other affairs, of other assignations. One such fling was with a fellow missionary when we were in language school together on the mission field!

They were both marathon runners and apparently did more than just running together! Learning more concretely of these affairs cemented the bricks of betrayal building around my heart. I still don't have the courage or strength to revisit those congregations, even though revisiting friends had always been a highlight of the past. The shame and humiliation of being the duped pastor's wife was too much.

What if one of those women who had desired my husband in the past came up to talk to me? I just couldn't do it.

Those congregations loved us. They trusted us. Though misplaced, I still felt like I was partially responsible for that betrayal, like I was a party to the sham. But the gospel we preached wasn't a sham! On the other hand, sympathetic looks and knowing glances would be unbearable as well. I felt like I had let them down, that I did not live up to the bargain of being a good enough pastor's wife. I visualize a sea of dear faces: the older women's Sunday school class that I taught and that made me a quilt, the young people's group that papered our home as a sign of acceptance, and the congregation we grew on the mission field. All that trust and adoration in their eyes and I wanted to hang my head in shame.

There must come a healing for them as well. I hate being responsible for their struggle to trust another pastor. Why should they listen to what any pastor has to say? They were probably thinking, "And his wife, she must have known what was going on all these years! How couldn't she?"

At the same time, I want to yell and scream, "I'm sorry. I'm so sorry for the betrayal from deep down in my innermost being, I'm sorry. I feel like I've turned my back and walked away from all of you." I feel a loneliness like I've never felt before, not of being physically alone, but of being alone in spirit, alienated, a setting-apart of my own doing. We said one thing and did another. In my thoughts, I have an image of me silhouetted against the surrounding darkness, the light from the open church door not quite reaching me.

Where were the written instructions on how to repair the damaged hearts after divorce? How had I arrived at this point in my life with the ground I'd always thought of as rock-solid melting from under my feet? I glance in the mirror and see a reasonably attractive middle-aged woman who only vaguely resembles the image of a younger self I carried around in my heart. The idealistic in-love college student/wife who traveled all over the world with her husband to minister in villages, towns, and cities.

Divorce irritates the wounds of many disappointed people who had looked up to us in the past. The only way that I could begin to heal with them was to simultaneously acknowledge our connectedness and our frailty. Our broken hearts together would have to hold hands across the globe like paper chains around a Christmas tree connecting families, churches, and individuals affected by this divorce. Together, we can pursue a change of heart toward forgiveness. What was my role in helping mend these hearts?

"Do you imagine that you, any more than they, will escape the judgment of God? Or do you think lightly of His wealth of kindness, of tolerance, and of patience, without recognizing that God's kindness is meant to lead you to a change of heart? In the rigid obstinacy of your heart, you are laying up for yourself a store of retribution for the day of retribution, when God's just judgment will be revealed, and He will pay every man for what he has done. To those who pursue glory, honor, and immortality by steady persistence in well doing, He will give eternal life. But for those who are governed by selfish ambition, who refuse obedience to the truth and take the wrong for their guide, there will be the fury of retribution. There will be trouble and distress for every human being who is an evil-doer, and for every well-doer there will be glory, honor, and peace." (Romans 2: 1–11)

I couldn't go back. If these congregants came to me, I would deal with those relationships as they showed themselves. I would tell the truth as needed, clarify confusing scenarios, and believe that they could work out their own feelings of betrayal.

Forgiveness
Chapter 6

Out of the depths have I called to thee, O Lord;
Lord, hear my cry.
Let thy ears be attentive to my pleas for mercy.
If thou, Lord, shouldest keep account of sins,
who, O Lord, could hold up his head?
But in thee is forgiveness,
and therefore, thou art revered.
I wait for the Lord with all my soul,
I hope for the fulfillment of his word.
My soul waits for the Lord
more eagerly than watchmen for the morning.
Psalms 130: 1–6

Today's sermon at church was on forgiveness. Sometimes, I absolutely hate church. It either makes me cry unabashedly or hardens my heart to the point that I do not want to listen. Today, I listened but did not absorb the message until after coming home. I let the words run around in my mind first before understanding what I needed to hear.

I came to a fragile epiphany; I can forgive him for replacing me. I understand his being dissatisfied. But, I cannot wrap my mind around his abandoning his children. I can know it, but I have not yet united the knowledge to understanding. Yes, they are grown, in that he no longer is legally responsible for them. He told them that he had a new family now and new responsibilities, that divorce was an issue between the two of us and didn't involve them. Divorce rips families apart and festers out to hurt everyone it touches. Adultery is an ugly, blinding seduction. It can only lead to more pain.

I have been stripped down after the divorce until there is nothing left. I want to be totally myself, determined and persistent in building up my children and myself. I felt at times trapped in a deep hole with stifling darkness. I did not have a sense of which direction was up. Day after day, the enemies within divorce assaulted me, making me think that I was helpless. I am starting to climb out of that hole, but sometimes my footing slips and the slide backwards can be precarious even while I'm assured that the danger is only temporary. I rely again and again on the Psalms for words of encouragement. It would be nice to have our own personal cheering squad rooting for us at every step, but we, as divorce survivors, can't depend on a squad to do the hard work for us. Diligence is ours to implement.

"I will exalt thee O Lord. Thou hast lifted me up and hast not let my enemies make merry over me. O Lord my God, I cried to thee and thou didst heal me. O Lord, thou hast brought me up from Sheol and saved my life as I was sinking into the abyss. Sing a psalm to the Lord, all you his royal servants, and give thanks to his holy name. In his anger is disquiet, in his favor there is life. Tears may linger at nightfall, but joy comes in the morning." (Psalms 30: 1–5)

Today's sermon emphasized the crucial ingredient of repentance in the formula of forgiveness. Have you ever been resistant to listening in church, even though you know that the sermon is just for you? That's how I felt today. My pastor talked about dying to my old self and allowing the new me to rise up in Christ. It is the first time that I have seen this lesson relate to me in this time of divorce. I have more than just permission to leave the old me behind: I am commanded to do so if I claim that Christ is really in me. This week would have been our 25th wedding anniversary and I am reminded again of loss and betrayal. How much more poignant and appropriate is this mandate of Christ's to put the old me aside and look for what is new and hopeful in Him ahead.

"Thus, says the Lord, who opened a way in the sea and a path through mighty waters, who drew on chariot and horse to their destruction, a whole army, men of valor, there they lay, never to rise again, they were crushed, snuffed out like a wick. Cease to dwell on days gone by and brood over past history. Here and now, I will do a new thing; this moment, it will break from the bud. Can you not perceive it? I will make a way even through the wilderness and paths in the barren desert." (Isaiah 43: 16–19)

My pastor talked about genealogies and the heritage of being a disciple of Christ, yet at the same time, not longing for how things used to be, but looking with hope to the future while being joyfully responsible for the present. I'm working on forgiving myself for not being the wife that Sam somehow needed, and I now realize that my promise to God to be committed to my husband was never broken, despite divorce. That is over and done with. I don't want to obey the spiritual darkness of wallowing in self-pity. Instead, I want to look with hope to the future while being joyfully responsible for the present.

Try asking yourself these questions: Have you abdicated the responsibility of how you handle each day? Are you just reacting to circumstances, or do you greet each day as a challenge? Are you weaving Christ into each decision that you make? I have choices. I can allow circumstances to overwhelm me or be pro-active and work with them. I can be full of self-pity and too weak to respond to daily interactions or be mindful of the dangers and rely on the Holy Spirit's constant guidance. It is up to me as to whether I incorporate Christ into each daily event or delegate Him to only points of desperation and need. My life must go on after divorce and I refuse to let mine continue without my full participation!

I'm not sure, but forgiveness in this situation for me is knowing with absolute assurance that Christ has forgiven or will forgive Sam for the sin of adultery, just as I have been forgiven and will continue to be so as I confess and ask for restoration.

This is tough because I really don't want to forgive Sam. I want to keep on re-telling the story of being a victim of adultery. It's an easily understood and accepted change of clothing to put on. Being a victim is a comfortable trench coat to wear. You don't have to adjust to inclement unexpected weather or shed layers to soak in warm sunshine. You can just continue to be and act in that same victim role, protected by the universal trench coat of the vindicated martyr. However, in always covering yourself up with the easy answers, you might end up abdicating your right to a fulfilling life that requires vulnerability. Because in shedding that protective coat, you reveal the layers of your own culpability in what happened!

Take me for an example. I did not stand up to Sam when he was sarcastic and ridiculed me. I allowed that abuse to continue. I also was an active participant in his justifying each move we made from church to church, from assignment to assignment. I consistently continued telling whatever story he asked me to tell. I willingly remained blind to what was going on around me. I didn't think I could stand up to the truth of his affairs. Now, post-divorce, I have the choice whether to wear the protection so readily available to me or not. I can shed all those entrapments by naming them and replacing them with honesty. That requires being vulnerable! Easy solutions and pat glib answers could no longer take the place of authenticity. I had work to do!

An immediate place to dig in and work is in the extended family dynamics. The root word of dynamics, dynamo, is appropriate because nothing blows up so easily as family relationships. We can't pretend that everything is OK now that adultery is all out in the open and legal. Just including the new post-divorce add-on marriage partners to the family birthday calendar or the Christmas exchange list is only a Band-Aid, a facade to continuing in a family and putting the divorce pain behind.

Extended family turbulence is one of the myriad natural consequences of affairs and remarriage. For example, my boys are struggling with accepting their dad's new wife and are also struggling with family members who have accepted her. They want to continue their relationship with their dad but have no desire to do so with Terry. I can understand how family members have a hard time accepting the add-on partner. If they do so, does that mean they are condoning adultery? This is a real and grueling dilemma that usually splits families apart.

I'm starting to recognize adultery in its rawness, that is, seeing it as it is, with no justification, with no allowances, with all its perverseness and selfishness, yet still trying to love the essence of the one who has done it in such a way that I am reconciled to the situation, but not to the person, the perpetrator of the adultery.

In that reconciliation, I am severed from the responsibility of deciphering, or understanding why the sin of adultery was committed against me and the boys in the first place. I choose not to be brought into the raucous emotional tug of war of how Sam resolves his issues. I cannot pretend that what he did to his family never happened, but we need healing much more than we need revenge or an airing of who was at fault. That type of ruminating only leads to disconnection from the source of healing, Jesus Christ.

I started healing by not continuing to force people to listen to my victimhood story. I had another story to tell. That story began with prayer. I don't want to sound trite about prayer, but it is a key to healing. Prayer is not a matter of a continuous wish list, but just a constant dialogue around the recognition of God's presence in our lives. The best metaphor I can think of is a tree trying to survive in a drought. Its leaves curl up on itself. It loses its vibrant color and droops towards the ground. When it rains, it sucks up that nourishment, unfurls its clenched leaves, returns to its intended vibrancy, and stands tall. Prayer does that for me.

Do you ever wake up one morning and realize that you haven't talked to God in days, have not considered His input? Sometimes, after a long drought of not voicing prayers, God's word will so move me that it loosens the rusted tap of prayer that I had believed frozen shut. A frenzied lament transforms into a sweet, sweet hour of prayer. God's word washes over me and cleanses me of all my perceived inadequacies. My face is scrubbed clean. I'm sitting in my garden. I angle towards the sun. The new day's warm rays greet me with expectation. I wonder what kept me away so long. Why did I wait? How could I forget the balm of God's word? I recommit again and again to the radiating source of His love, His word. And you know, He understands my failings and doesn't mind my having to reconnect repeatedly. I return in all honesty and with no pretenses.

"Then away with all malice and deceit, away with all pretense and jealousy and recrimination of every kind. Like newborn infants you are, you must crave for pure milk (spiritual milk, I mean), so that you may thrive upon it to your souls' health. Surely, you have tasted that the Lord is good. So, come to Him, our living Stone—the stone rejected by men but choice and precious in the sight of God. Come, and let yourselves be built, as living stones, into a spiritual temple; become a holy priesthood, to offer spiritual sacrifices acceptable to God through Jesus Christ." (1 Peter 2: 1–6)

We each individually face God's judgment daily, so why waste precious healing energy worrying about another's repentance? Yet, by no means does forgiveness mean acceptance and condoning of the sin. I am grateful my Lord will continue forgiving me. My road to recovery rests on my repentance, which means turning purposefully towards a different path where I claim my freedom from the power Sam had to continually hurt me. It is a conscious choice that I must make repeatedly every day. I wonder if down the line, at that magical five-year marker that the books and counselors espouse is the time needed to get over a divorce, my obsession with fear of being hurt will be gone, the wounds of divorce be only scars?

The abrupt cessation of making memories with a life partner is one of the casualties of divorce. What makes memories so precious is that if they're not handled carefully, they fall apart. I've been working on scrapbooking during some slow days this summer. My sister gave me a gift certificate to a scrapbooking class to help me feel better. She knows me well! This simple act of cutting and pasting, gluing and arranging has rekindled in me the joy of family memories and the joy of creativity. These pictures and memorabilia will become artifacts of life in this family especially after divorce. For we are still a family with precious memories and comforting traditions, such a simple revelation, but a moment of clarity for me.

One parent or two living together, we nevertheless remain family, determined to strengthen those bonds and not face life frightened and suspicious of eminent unraveling. I will count my blessings of family, celebrate die-hard traditions, and gleefully anticipate the metamorphosis of new memories. I will do these things because, "Honor and dishonor, praise and blame, are alike our lot. We are the impostors who speak the truth, the unknown men whom all men know; dying we still live on; disciplined by suffering, we are not done to death. In our sorrows, we have always cause for joy; poor ourselves, we bring wealth to many; penniless, we own the world." (2 Corinthians 6: 6–12)

Two of my sanctuaries have been church and the members of my family. I can't recall when worship wasn't part of every fiber of my life. Morning worship around the breakfast table as a child was a ritual that I counted on yet hated at the same time for its inconvenience. Stories, songs, and prayers were told, read, and sung to me from my older siblings, mother, nanny, Sunday school teachers, and others. You would have been hard pressed to find anyone in my life who didn't love the Lord and express that love during every turn of every day.

Sunday worship was just a continuation of the rest of the week. Sermons were dissected, criticized, and praised, and songs were learned, hummed, and repeated. We jumped rope and played hopscotch in rhythm to choruses. We washed dishes and swept floors listening to songs of the heart. None in my family were exceptionally musical, but we made plenty of joyful noises banging away on the piano or listening to worn out records. Don't get me wrong, we weren't ultra-spiritual, conservative, or 'holier than thou.' It was just a matter of fact that the Lord was why my parents did what they did, why we lived where we lived, and why we were raised the way we were.

Church was always there. There were some sermons that were so long and boring that I thought the preacher would never shut up, or like my grandmother would say, "he talks just to hear his head rattle!" There were some special music numbers that I was sure weren't even sweet and special to the Lord! Yet, other services carried me even as a child straight to the angels. All of this to say that worship with my husband had been integral to our love for each other and came straight from the heart, so I thought.

I was proud of the first time I heard him preach when he was being licensed at his grandparent's church, the same church in which we eventually married. That first sermon was too long as so many firsts are, yet I was right there with him, agonizing over every word. While in college, I would go with him on Sundays, as he would practice preaching in small congregations near our university town. I remember after we married, one church specifically, the little congregation was so pleased with his preaching that they wanted him to come every Sunday. However, the drawback was me. I couldn't play the piano or sing specials! Imagine a pastor's wife who wasn't musical! We used to laugh about these funny-shared experiences.

Our first pastorate was the dearest group of people who still keep up with me today. The church was the typical white frame building, with beautifully carved wooden pews. The parsonage perched on the corner across the street from both the church and the school on the other side. We were financially poor, but rich in life. He was finishing up his seminary work and I taught school while we were in the missionary application process and pastoring that church. Both our children were born while we lived in that parsonage where water froze in the kitchen sink in the winter and the curtains billowed with the windows closed!

What about the unsurpassed joy of growing a congregation from scratch on the mission field? Our life's dream goal of being missionaries together, learning and working, failing and growing, was being activated. Even with personal trials of family illness and uncertainties, we weathered the storms and worshipped the Lord together on the mission field.

Later came the subsequent pastorates here in the States. I always felt that we were partners in ministry as well as marriage. Church politics, financial strains, and medical dilemmas attacked us, but we always turned to each other and together to our Lord for support. I'm not trying to paint an idyllic picture, just punctuating the moments I thought were authentic worship through the years. As people would compliment his preaching and leadership, I always responded with, "even though he is my husband, he's also my favorite pastor."

I have acutely missed my worship partner. I miss the sharing of the nuances of worship, of rehashing a sermon over Sunday lunch, of holding hands in a particularly moving musical rendition, of feeling the swell of joint pride when one of our boys commented on an aspect of a service. That's one of the angles of marriage that I long for the most: worshipping with the one I love. Why am I recounting memories? Because precious memories make forgiveness hard work. You feel like you've lost so much that anger at losing anymore annihilates the possibility of forgiveness.

For months after the divorce, I couldn't go to church at all. Before the secret of the affair was out, I couldn't stand the heaviness of subterfuge. Then after the ugly sordidness became public knowledge, I couldn't receive graciously the sympathy and words of condolences. Easter was torture because I didn't feel resurrected and new, but haggard and used. Christmas was agonizing as families joined hands for the 'hanging of the green.' I still fortify myself with tissues each Sunday and enter worship with trepidation, hoping I won't make a fool of myself again with a show of tears. As the husband of one of my friends said one Sunday, "Haven't you gotten over this divorce thing yet?" A question like that is asked out of the coziness of marriage and I'm sure he didn't realize the painful extent of that dagger of words.

Yet, I continued attending the same church as before divorce. It was my church. Those were my people. Sam didn't attend there much because he was routinely doing interim pastorates and guest speaking. By the way, I found out later that money he received from these engagements, he put in a secret bank account so that he could use it on his many personal wants. I say this as an example of my own blindness to happenings under my own nose. I chose to be blind so as not to be on the receiving end of accusations of mistrust.

It's tough work not letting the erosion of divorce crumble the tower of strength I used to have in worship. Private worship is my safe sanctuary now. I don't abandon public worship, but I have to re-approach it with caution, being mindful of the land mines of emotion inherent in it. My love for the Lord has not been stolen from me, just reshaped by the chisels of betrayal. Worship cannot ever be a luxury for me, but a base of survival. Even having to return to the Lord repeatedly can be an integral part of our worship.

My incessant and fervent prayer during that first year of divorce was: "Lord, give me routine and boredom. Please, no more emotional roller coaster rides, no more upheavals. I'm tired of character development!" Then when the solitude of routine was firmly entrenched, I started complaining yet again, only to realize that no matter what my emotional circumstances, the living out of Christ's character was to be paramount in my life.

Godly habits are exercised by my willing them to be so, not by them supernaturally happening. I can't expect to be His star pupil every minute of every day, but I can expect to exhibit the results of His grace in my ordinary life. He is my essence. Routine and boring drudgery can be the vehicle for developing genuine character. The routine of life can be our

Lord's method of rejuvenating and saving us for those eventual times of draining trauma. I must live in the knowledge that my obedience in routine has all the omnipotent power of the grace of God. Take advantage of God's grace and bask in the healing waters of routine.

Through the vehicle of obedient routine, I learned to drive out self-recrimination. I am now able to recognize the roadblocks where I didn't forgive myself. The road crew of family, friends, and church community helped remove those roadblocks and I've been able to continue my journey of healing forgiveness.

"Come let us return to the Lord, for He has torn us and will heal us. He has struck us and He will bind up our wounds. After two days, He will revive us. On the third day, He will restore us, that in His presence, we may live. Let us humble ourselves, let us strive to know the Lord, whose justice dawns like morning light, and its dawning is as sure as the sunrise. It will come to us like a shower, like spring rains that water the earth." (Hosea 6: 1–3)

Hope
Chapter 7

Knowing that you possessed something better and more
lasting.
Do not then throw away your confidence,
for it carries a great reward.
You need endurance,
if you are to do God's will and win what he has promised...
But we are not among those who shrink back and are lost;
we have the faith to make life our own.
Hebrews 10:34–36, 39

I am teetering between melancholy over love lost and
anticipation of God's provision.

Disillusionment is a recurring theme in the psyche of a
divorced woman. Even though we have broken free from the
deceptive tentacles of a crumbled marriage and are no longer
under the false pretenses of a life-long commitment, I doubt
if we have let go of the resulting cynicism. I know I find
myself suspicious and doubtful of men in general. I find
myself doubting sincerity and honesty in relationships,
constantly over-scrutinizing and analyzing, wondering if
deception is lurking around the corner. This type of behavior
is so unfair.

How would I feel knowing that people were cynically
judging me, doubting my sincerity, questioning my motives?
Just because my idealism was shattered does not give me the
right to drape disillusionment like a shroud on each
subsequent relationship. May the Lord forgive me of my sin
of cynicism and help me to trust Him to instead see people

realistically through His eyes. 1 Peter 2:15–17 sums it up for me. "For it is the will of God that by your good conduct, you should put ignorance and stupidity to silence. Live as free men, not however as though your freedom were there to provide a screen for wrongdoing, but as slaves in God's service. Give due honor to everyone; love to the brotherhood, reverence to God, honor to the sovereign."

It's as if God is aiming at something I can't see. He goes on stretching me until His purpose is in sight for that particular situation, then He lets the arrow fly. I will throw myself with abandon and total confidence upon Him. I have been stripped down this year until there is nothing left. I want to be totally myself, determined and persistent toward encouraging and building up my boys, family, and friends.

Right on the pinnacle of a high emotion like finishing my doctorate, or launching my sons into the world, I savor the glowing enthusiasm of success. Then I feel myself sliding because that one who used to participate in my joy is gone. I am assailed by disappointment because Sam is not there to sustain me in dejection. Someday, maybe, will I have another companion?

I would like the luxury of the company of one who can understand me, whose eyes can reply to mine. I want someone with me, a gentle yet courageous companion, possessed of a cultivated as well as capricious mind, giving and kind, and loving me for who I am—not with an agenda of how I can be altered to fit his needs. I have a love for the spiritual. I need a companion to match or exceed my ardor. I have a love for the marvelous, a belief in the miraculous, intertwined in all my projects, which hurries me out of the common pathways, even into the scary unknown, the ambiguous regions of the future. Is this too much to ask? Then, I have interruptions in the routine of life. Interruptions that let me know that there is hope for this replaced old gal!

Habitually, on Sundays, I like to visit the bagel shop before Sunday school and read for a while. I am cursed and blessed with the gift of organization. My body doesn't know that it doesn't have to get up at five on Saturday and Sunday, but it does anyway, with the help of my cat who nibbles on my nose if I don't get a move on. I'm up and dressed with no place to go until 9:30 for Sunday school, so I take myself to the bagel shop to muse away the morning.

There I was settled in my favorite booth, away from the flow of traffic, lost in the throes of the favorite 'book of the week.' A shadow passed over my pages. I glanced up to see 'a tall, dark, and handsome, stranger' smiling and saying good morning to me! I must have looked totally confused, trying to separate from my book, and I stutteringly uttered a garbled, "Good morning."

He lingered at my table and started speaking again. "I don't know how to say this, but I've noticed you in here before, and have waited for the courage to introduce myself to you."

My thoughts responded with, *what! Noticed me—like in, you look good and maybe even interesting. That's remarkable!*

"I've looked for a wedding ring and I think your ring is not one and you're always in here alone. Can I assume that you're single?" he asked.

"Why yes, I am," I managed to reply.

"Do you live here?" he continued.

And the conversation took off from there.

At an attempt for witticism, I asked, "But can I assume since you're asking me these questions, you're single too?"

He chuckled. I was startled at the pleasant sound and thought, *You mean, I'm not only worth noticing, but say amusing things as well? What do you know?*

We continued visiting and he commented that no matter how old you get, this initiating a conversation is a difficult thing to do, especially if your intention is to ask for a phone number. Where my brave move came from next I do not know. And apparently, I do have my wits about me and can have coherent thoughts occasionally, for I asked him to join me for a cup of coffee. We exchanged phone numbers and he called later that week. I had a delightful time on a date with him.

It wasn't my first time going out since the divorce. My dear, concerned brother-in-law had set me up twice and both men have been charming, and I went out with them several times. But, this time was different, someone was attracted to me on my own merit. I know that you hear constantly and read repeatedly that when a husband leaves, it's not about you but about him. However, to internalize that, to believe it, is a monumental struggle. That abscessed, rotten feeling of rejection is like having your heart ripped out, tossed in the street, and cars run over it back and forth, while he stands on the sidewalk watching, aloof, removed, and with arms crossed over his chest.

No wonder dating again seems like such an insurmountable, 'no way in hell am I going to do that again' kind of experience.

Am I good enough? is a nagging question, since harbored at the pit of my stomach is the feeling that I wasn't good enough before. Is there any inkling that I could possibly be good enough again?

I am learning to take responsibility for my own feelings and I've started by deliberately adjusting my surroundings to fit myself. The first step was changing my name back to my maiden name, which I think upset my ex-in-laws, but it was a baby step towards claiming my independence. Next, I went through each room in the house and sifted through what Sam had left behind. The boys claimed what they wanted, his family picked up some, and the rest I gave away. Something as simple as buying pink towels and a flowered shower curtain jumpstarted my self-esteem quotient. I sold our wedding pottery and bought new dishes, changed wallpaper and rearranged furniture, dug a rose garden and added perennials. The front shutters, I had painted sunshine yellow and the outside fixtures went from dull iron black to golden brass. People would slow down in their cars as they passed my house and would comment on the facelift of my home.

Speaking of facelifts, my appearance has changed so drastically that people I've known and haven't seen for a while walk right by me and don't recognize me until I speak.

I lost weight, cut and highlighted my hair, and revamped my wardrobe with the help of my sewing machine and a tailor. My niece even decided that I needed a new scent and went with me to pick out a signature perfume for Aunt Sheila! I go to the movies that I want to go to, go to bed as early as I please, and wake up with the dawn. Those used to be big issues with us. I've always loved the very early morning hours and was rebuked by Sam for my preference.

Each step has been minuscule, but combined with the others, served to announce to me and the world that my former spouse no longer had the right to define who I was. I no longer needed his approval to cut my hair or not, or anything else for that matter. I am knowing who I am and no longer need to measure my worth by his expectations.

Without a husband, I became frenetic. I baked and cleaned, and decorated. I dug flowerbeds, weeded, and painted. It was infinitely comforting to get in touch with my house and things. I remembered how I felt when we acquired each item, so full of anticipation of life shared together. I thought to myself, *Look at me efficiently moving through the furniture of my life, what a good wife and mother I am. My price is surely above rubies.* And then with a jolt, I am hurled back into reality. I am no longer a wife—good or otherwise. I would spend long lapses perusing memorabilia of days gone by, giving brief and temporary solace to a breaking heart. I know that my only solace comes from the Lord and that things are just temporary. Maybe I was trying to caress the memories of what these belongings evoked in me. And yet, I was doing this working of sorting out because I did have hope.

"The light of day is sweet, and pleasant to the eye is the sight of the sun. If a man lives for many years, he should rejoice in all of them. But let him remember that the days of darkness will be many. Everything that is to come will be emptiness. Delight in your childhood, make the most of the days of your youth, let your heart and your eyes show you the way, but remember that for all these things, God will call you to account. Banish discontent from your mind and shake off the troubles of the body. Childhood and the prime of life are mere emptiness. This is the end of the matter; you have heard it all. Fear God and obey His commands; there is no more to man than this. For God brings everything we do to judgment, and every secret, whether good or bad." (Ecclesiastes 11:7–10, 12: 1314)

Through Sam's act of adultery and leaving our marriage, he wiped out the familial record of continuity sustained by memories and hoped for future experiences. What I had held as precious and worth preserving, he devalued and replaced. Therefore, I had to choose to disengage from the objects and people that inhabited those memories. For example, soon after the divorce, my ex-in-laws asked me over to their home for dinner.

I declined and explained that the memories were too raw and painful, but that I would be glad to meet them at a restaurant for dinner. We did that, but they have never asked me again. The truth can't be vindicated. So, the wedding dress that I beaded myself is saved as a historical relic and fashion statement, and the wedding album is stored along with the baby books as a legitimate item in the family archives if the children want them later. I had in the past taken on the role of illustrating the definition of our family by way of keeping family traditions and albums. However, even that role was changing.

My healing not only depends on my physical house cleaning and makeovers, but also on my emotional cobweb sweeping. I cannot stifle my recovery because others refuse to go along with it or disapprove of my nerve. I must instead confront each fear, each lie, and each morsel of pity, and claim my freedom from them, no matter how painful the process. I re-take my thoughts, which had been taken captive by a manipulating, and yes abusive husband, a man who used lies to promote his own agenda and defend his adultery.

I've read books that tell me I must pray for the one that hurt me and that I must release him to God's judgment and mercy. They audaciously give me little gimmicky exercises with helium balloons to represent the letting go of the old life. Even the Bible tells me repeatedly to pray for my enemies. I'm not there yet. I do better by just putting him out of my mind. Others tell me that they're praying for him. That's good. I'm still too deep in the throes of his hurt to pray for him in all sincerity. For our love was the evidence of real communication, the certain proof that the feeling within myself had broken its bonds of flesh. It reached out and found, and awakened the same feeling in another, as two people will talk in darkness, understanding. That's what I had previously thought anyway. Now I was beginning to know better.

To replace that void of emptiness where love used to live are the wonderful girlfriends that give hope for recovery. They give hope because in their vulnerability and weakness, I recognized myself. I saw their successes and triumphs through adversity and knew then that I could do likewise.

Besides my private sanctuary of worship, my sisters and girlfriends have probably been the most influential in my healing process. I profoundly appreciate their help in rebuilding my sense of self with stern remarks, ribald humor, gentle coaxing, and silent understanding. God put a group of precious friends in my life in the very year that I needed them the most. We religiously meet once a month for dinner out and claim a booth or table for several hours of exuberant hilarity and/or tear-soaked confidences.

We are a conglomeration of still married, remarried, almost married, and unmarried. We have covenanted to be there for each other and we are. My card collection from these women is funny, poignant, heart wrenching, and comforting. We make a huge deal out of each one of our birthdays and find any occasion to celebrate a happening! I can call anyone of them day or night and they are there for me. With my family not nearby, my girlfriends have more than stepped in and been my mother and sisters combined. There is not a single thing that they do not know about me, and I am confidently covered by their prayers daily. Survival this year would have been impossible without them. They have been God's personal precious gift to me and I hope to have ample opportunities to repay them for their generosity.

Nevertheless, I have placed an inordinate amount of pressure on my network to get me through post-divorce. I have expected them to feel sorry for me, no matter how much time has lapsed since the divorce. At the very moment of needy commiserating, I find myself insisting on their emotional cooperation. I have expected them to pick me up and put my life together for me or at least put together whatever broken pieces I have so graciously dumped in their laps. Within our relationships of vulnerability and trust, I have implied that I'm expecting them to do my emotional dirty work for me. This does not work though. I have to do the heavy lifting myself. They are just my cheering squad.

Telling the truth about my pain of experiencing adultery has freed me to be authentic and authoritatively content in my own presence. I have struggled these last two years to vindicate the truth, only to know now that instead, I must clutch tightly to what I know to be true and fix my eyes on God, the 'author and finisher' of my life. No one else gets to have the privilege of being the author of me, except the partnership of me and God Almighty!

References

New English Bible, Cambridge, At the University Press, Great Britain, 1972.